7/06

The Music
Library

The History of Jazz

Other books in this series include:

The Music
Library

The History of Jazz

by Stuart A. Kallen

LUCENT
BOOKS®

THOMSON
★
GALE

San Diego • Detroit • New York • San Francisco • Cleveland • New Haven, Conn. • Waterville, Maine • London • Munich

THOMSON

———— ✶ ————

GALE

LIBRARY OF CONGRESS CATALOGING-IN-PUBLICATION DATA

Kallen, Stuart A., 1955–
    The history of jazz / by Stuart A. Kallen.
       v. cm. — (The music library)
Includes bibliographical references (p.) and index.
Summary: Discusses the origins of jazz, famed jazz musicians, musical movements within the genre, and jazz's influence on rock 'n' roll.
Contents: Introduction: "Never played the same way once" — The roots of jazz — The swingin' jazz age — Dancing to swing — The birth of bebop — The cool, the hard, and the free — Fusion and beyond.
    ISBN 1-59018-125-5 (alk. paper)
    1. Jazz—History and criticism—Juvenile literature. [1. Jazz—History and criticism.]
I. Title. II. Music library (San Diego, Calif.)
    ML3506 .K35 2003
    781.65'09—dc21

                                       2002002220

Printed in the United States of America

• Contents •

• Foreword •

In the nineteenth century English novelist Charles Kingsley wrote, "Music speaks straight to our hearts and spirits, to the very core and root of our souls. . . . Music soothes us, stirs us up . . . melts us to tears." As Kingsley stated, music is much more than just a pleasant arrangement of sounds. It is the resonance of emotion, a joyful noise, a human endeavor that can soothe the spirit or excite the soul. Musicians can also imitate the expressive palate of the earth, from the violent fury of a hurricane to the gentle flow of a babbling brook.

The word music is derived from the fabled Greek muses, the children of Apollo who ruled the realms of inspiration and imagination. Composers have long called upon the muses for help and insight. Music is not merely the result of emotions and pleasurable sensations, however.

Music is a discipline subject to formal study and analysis. It involves the juxtaposition of creative elements such as rhythm, melody, and harmony with intellectual aspects of composition, theory, and instrumentation. Like painters mixing red, blue, and yellow into thousands of colors, musicians blend these various elements to create classical symphonies, jazz improvisations, country ballads, and rock-and-roll tunes.

Throughout centuries of musical history, individual musical elements have been blended and modified in infinite ways. The resulting sounds may convey a whole range of moods, emotions, reactions, and messages. Music, then, is both an expression and reflection of human experience and emotion.

The foundations of modern musical styles were laid down by the first ancient musicians who used wood, rocks, animal skins—and their own bodies—to re-create the sounds of the natural world in which they lived. With their hands, their feet, and their very breath they ignited the passions of listeners and moved them to their feet. The dancing, in turn, had a mesmerizing and hypnotic effect that allowed people to transcend their worldly concerns. Through music they could achieve a level of shared experience that could not be found in other forms of communication. For this reason, music has always been part of religious endeavors, from ancient Egyptian religious ceremonies to modern Christian masses. And it has inspired dance movements from kings and queens spinning the minuet to punk rockers slamming together in a mosh pit.

By examining musical genres ranging from Western classical music to rock and roll, readers will find a new understanding of old music and develop an appreciation for new sounds. Books in Lucent's Music Library focus on the music, the musicians, the instruments, and on music's place in cultural history. The songs and artists examined may be easily found in the CD and sheet music collections of local libraries so that readers may study and enjoy the music covered in the books. Informative sidebars, annotated bibliographies, and complete indexes highlight the text in each volume and provide young readers with many opportunities for further discussion and research.

Introduction

"Never Played the Same Way Once"

Jazz music is everywhere. People hear it in movies, on the radio and television, and even playing from overhead speakers in grocery stores. Millions of people buy jazz CDs every year, and musicians play jazz in concert halls, barrooms, and theaters throughout the world.

As popular as jazz is around the world, its roots are distinctly American. The beginnings of jazz music can be traced to New Orleans, Louisiana, at the end of the nineteenth century. There, African American musicians blended several forms of traditional music, including work songs, field hollers, blues, ragtime, Mardi Gras marches, and European military music, to create a completely new sound.

At first this new music was called ragtime, possibly because of its "ragged" rhythms. By the 1920s the sound was labeled jass, or jazz. The origins of the word are unclear, but legend has it that *jazz* was used in New Orleans as a euphemism for *sex*. The word was commonly used in the houses of prostitution that lined the streets of the notorious Storyville district where musicians played night after night. Some historians believe, however, that the word may have originally meant "hurry up," and was first used by Afro-Caribbean musicians who instructed their bands to play faster by saying "Jazz it up!"[1]

Whatever the origins of the word, *jazz* soon became a vital part of the American vocabulary, and the word was used to describe anything that was fashionable or trendy, including cars, clothes, and even an entire decade: The wild years between 1920 and 1930 are known as the Jazz Age.

Swinging and Jamming

Although *jazzy* may be used to describe anything that is especially bright, new, or different, it has a very specific meaning when applied to music. Most jazz music is defined by three main elements: swing, improvisation, and a distinctive voice. Swing is the driving rhythmic beat that makes people want to dance, clap along, or tap their feet. This feeling is so important that jazz composer Duke Ellington immortalized it in his song "It Don't Mean a Thing (If It Ain't Got That Swing)."

Jazz musicians can make the music swing by playing with the beat of the music. Most early jazz was played in a steady repetitive beat, known as 4/4 time because there are four beats to every measure. When the players hit a note a little before or slightly after the beat, the music has what is known as syncopation. When this happens, the music is described by players as "swinging," or having an "edge" or "groove." And by accenting the off-beats, musicians can create different grooves. When playing slightly after the beat, musicians can get a "laid-back" or soulful sound. By playing before the beat, the music can sound surprising or exciting and put listeners on the edge of their seats—or make them get up and dance.

Jazz musicians also thrive on improvisation—that is, they improvise or make up melodies on the spot rather than reading them from previously written music scores. As they create connections between musical passages, known as "riffs" or "licks," to form a steady stream of jazz music, players are said to develop their "chops."

Improvising is also known as "jamming" or "ad-libbing." When jazz musicians jam, they compose and play at the same time, taking turns playing solos.

This allows individual players in a group to show off their musical skills and creativity. Jazz players believe an infinite number of melodies can be played within any song. As jazz legend Louis Armstrong once joked, "Jazz is music that's never played the same way once."[2]

Improvisers often imitate singing with their instruments, gliding, swooping, and soaring through seemingly endless cascades of notes. Musicians (especially horn players) may "bend" notes (wavering between two different tones) to obtain a "blues" quality or make their instrument growl and wail to imitate a type of singing known as "scat." Whatever a player does, however, he or she tries to be original, artistic, and imaginative.

The best jazz players aspire to create a unique sound, or "voice," that is provided by their tone, their creative selection of notes, and their overall rhythm. For example, many jazz fans can easily differentiate the playing of Miles Davis from other trumpeters or identify the saxophone of Charlie Parker because of the individual voices these musicians possess. Good jazz is music that expresses feelings and emotion, and the musician's voice is a product of his or her deep emotional state. The players and the audience might be moved to joy, sadness, exhilaration, introspection, or any combination of these emotions.

The Diversity of America

Just as jazz reflects the wide-ranging emotions of the musicians, it also reflects the diversity of America's music scene. Long before integration between the races became a goal in American society, black and white jazz musicians played together on stage. In the years before women became a powerful political force, female vocalists such as Ella Fitzgerald and Billie Holiday became living icons of independent, free-thinking women. And jazz musicians had a lasting effect on American music in general. As musician and producer Quincy Jones writes, "Jazz has left an indelible handprint on America's history, a central thread woven through the fabric of our country. Morphing itself, and giv-ing birth to a host of other musical genres . . . [it] is part of the bedrock of pop [music], R&B [rhythm and blues], and rock music, and it's an intricate road map to our culture."[3]

It is this diversity that makes jazz true American music, providing every fan with something to love. People who do not appreciate the often cacophonous sounds of "free jazz" might swing to the historic sounds of Louis Armstrong's Hot Five band. Those who disregard the orchestral sounds of the big-band era may love the driving improvisation of bebop. Some who reject early twentieth-century ragtime might find solace in the

Jazz singers such as Billie Holiday (right) became symbols of empowered, free-thinking women.

jazz-rock fusion that has been popular since the 1970s.

Once heard mostly in the smoky barrooms of New Orleans, Kansas City, and Chicago, today jazz music represents the creative musical side of the United States to people across the globe. Jazz personalities such as Miles Davis, Louis Armstrong, Billie Holiday, and others are heroes to countless jazz fans from Tokyo to Paris to New Delhi.

Just as a swinging jazz quartet unites its individual players behind a driving syncopated beat, jazz music has proven its ability to bring people together over a shared interest in a universal sound. As singer Tony Bennett writes, "Jazz is spontaneous, honest, and natural, and it is a celebration of life itself."[4]

Chapter One

The Roots of Jazz

At the end of the 1800s New Orleans was one of the most exciting cities in the United States, standing at a crossroads for American, French, African, and Caribbean cultures. The local music reflected that diversity. Like gumbo, the spicy seafood stew that has long been a favorite of the local citizens, the music of New Orleans was a blend of various ingredients that inspired people to always come back for more.

New Orleans was originally established by France around 1718, and the French citizens who settled in the city had a strong affinity for the arts and music. By the end of the eighteenth century, for example, the city had three opera companies, two symphony orchestras, countless theaters, and several French-language newspapers. So culturally sophisticated was the city that after the region became part of the United States in 1803, New Orleans was referred to as "the Paris of America."[5]

The residents of New Orleans were sophisticated, but they also loved to parade and party. Every spring residents celebrated the Mardi Gras holiday during a carnival season that lasted six to eight weeks. The Mardi Gras festival, based on an ancient Christian tradition, featured costumes, parades, and marching bands—a tradition that continues.

For all of their sophistication, the French were also participants in the slave trade, and tens of thousands of black people who had been kidnapped in West Africa passed through the city on their way to plantations throughout the South. New Orleans was also home to many free blacks who worked as household servants or skilled artisans. These people, who made up about 20 percent of the city's population during the early 1800s, created a thriving black subculture.

When slavery ended in 1865, after the Civil War, New Orleans became one of the centers of black culture in the United States and acted as a magnet for black people throughout the southern states as well as those living in South America and Caribbean islands such as Haiti, Cuba, and Jamaica. Many of the Haitians were of mixed African and French ancestry and were known as Creoles. The light-skinned Creoles identified more closely with European culture than with African or black southern cultures, and those who were musicians were often classically trained. These individuals found inspiration not just in the musical traditions of the Caribbean but also in the music of Bach, Beethoven, and Mozart.

The multicultural mix in New Orleans was further swelled by sailors from around the world whose ships passed through the bustling port of New Orleans—the second busiest in North America. As a major seaport and a popular tourist destination, New Orleans catered to crowds who were eager to be entertained. As a result, the streets of the city were lined with bars, brothels, and theaters. The city's free-wheeling lifestyle did not sit well with everyone, however, and in 1897 a conservative city alderman named Charles Story drafted legislation to confine prostitution to one specific neighborhood, an area that soon became known, ironically, as Storyville.

The owners of the brothels contributed greatly to the development of the city's musical tradition by hiring

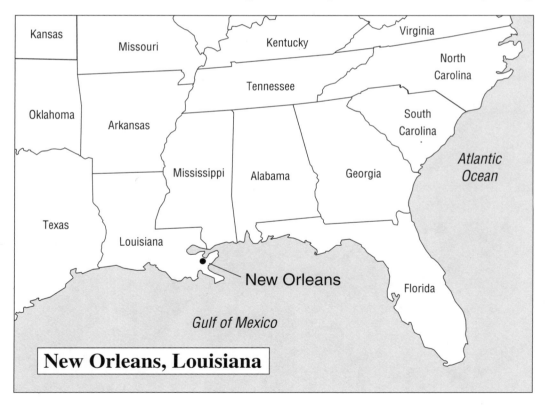

New Orleans, Louisiana

musicians to entertain their clients. By the beginning of the twentieth century there were more than 175 places in Storyville where musicians could find work. In addition, New Orleans had hundreds of bars, restaurants, and theaters that catered to the tourist trade. As a result, the city attracted skilled musicians from across the United States, Europe, and the Caribbean.

This cultural conglomeration yielded an unprecedented mix of musical sounds. As Mark C. Gridley writes in *Jazz Styles: History and Analysis,*

New Orleans was a whirlwind of musical activity. Diverse styles were in the air. Opera coexisted with sailor's hornpipes. Music for the European dances of the minuet and quadrille coexisted with African music used in [Haitian] voodoo ceremonies. Band music in the style of . . . [marching band composer] John Philip Sousa [was] quite popular. There were also the work songs of the laborers and the musical cries of street vendors selling their wares.[6]

In this festive atmosphere, it is no wonder New Orleans earned the nickname "the Big Easy," and its motto became *laissez les bons temps roulez,* or "let the good times roll."

A Mardi Gras celebration in 19th century New Orleans. The city's festive atmosphere attracted scores of aspiring musicians.

The African Root of Jazz

When jazz was born, millions of black people were living in the American South, and most of them were either former slaves or were descended from former slaves. These people could trace their roots to West Africa, where music with many similarities to jazz had been played for centuries.

Like jazz, ancient African tribal music had several defining factors: It featured a strong drumbeat, improvised licks, voices imitating instruments, and the use of short, repeated phrases of melody (later called "riffs" by jazz musicians). In addition, African music was based on a technique known as call and response, in which a song leader would sing a line and a group of singers would repeat that line. This improvised music was passed from generation to generation by "ear"—that is, without written scores.

The drum is central to African music, and like jazz, the syncopated, or "swing," rhythm is highly valued. African drummers also create music by using several different rhythms and beats that weave around and intertwine with each other, a technique known as polyrhythm.

In addition to drums, African musicians played horns, trumpets, and several types of stringed instruments, including the *banjar,* the forerunner to the modern banjo that was adapted for use in ragtime, jazz, and other music.

Spirituals and the Blues

Musicians in New Orleans mixed the ancient musical traditions of Africa with those found in the New World. For example, many blacks in the South were accustomed to religious songs called spirituals. These featured the call-and-response format that dated back to African tribal music in which a leader would sing a verse and the congregation would repeat it in unison. Black musicians in New Orleans composed their own spirituals, adding "swing" rhythms and bent-note blues melodies.

This call-and-response style was also found in work songs that laborers sang while picking cotton, hoeing crops, building fences, and so on. Known as field hollers or blues hollers, these songs were heard wherever people labored together in groups.

Forced to work at the most physically demanding jobs, southern blacks also faced relentless prejudice and poverty. The pain and frustration of their condition found a voice in blues songs that dealt with themes such as loneliness, poverty, homelessness, and discrimination. These songs, called twelve-bar blues because they feature twelve measures of music per verse, would be incorporated into the music that came to be known as jazz.

Strutting to Ragtime

Life was not all blues, however, and on Sundays, when they did not have to go to work, people tended to get together after church to sing and dance. In *Introduction to Jazz History,* Donald D. Megill and Richard S. Demory write about an entertainment known as cakewalk:

> A favorite Sunday amusement [for African Americans] was parodying European dances that they had seen the white gentry performing at balls and socials. These parody-dances were accompanied by syncopated tunes played on fiddles and banjos; they usually included a "walka-round," in which couples would parade around a square and improvise high-stepping, vigorous movements as they turned each corner. These entertainments were often performed before whites and were incorporated . . . in minstrel shows. Couples who were judged to be the most inventive would receive a prize, often a cake. Thus, the strutting,

high-kicking dance to syncopated music became known as the *cakewalk.* In the 1890s the cakewalk craze swept the country; whites from coast to coast cakewalked. And so another double deception occurred, only in this case whites imitated blacks who were mimicking whites. [7]

The preferred music at cakewalk dances was known as ragtime, invented by musicians who introduced syncopation to a song to make the rhythm ragged. By the 1890s pianists were composing complicated ragtime songs in which the player's right hand "tickled" the keys with a strong rhythmic melody while the left hand played an intricate bass part. Although these complex melodies were often written down on sheet music, some players embellished existing scores with improvised licks.

The most famous ragtime piece, "Maple Leaf Rag," was written by Texas-born composer Scott Joplin in 1899. The song was written before the era of recorded music, but "Maple Leaf Rag" sold up to half a million copies in the form of sheet music in a few short years. The popularity of Joplin's composition started a national ragtime fad, and by the 1920s nearly every bar and brothel in the United States featured ragtime ensembles composed of singers, trumpet players, banjo players, drummers, and pianists. In fact, before the term *jazz* came into common use during the 1920s, most jazz players considered themselves ragtime musicians.

European Influence

The final musical ingredients of the New Orleans musical gumbo were the brass bands and marching bands of European origin. These bands featured trumpets, trombones, tubas, and drums, and they were extremely popular throughout the United States at the end of the nineteenth century. New Orleans boasted dozens of these ensembles, each with over twelve members. The musicians in the New Orleans marching bands were almost exclusively black, and they played at events both happy and sad, such as church dances, Mardi Gras celebrations, and funerals. In 1909 one unnamed witness recalled the sight of a brass band marching down his street:

> Suddenly, from around the corner marched these colored men. Oh, they walked so tall and stiff. Bright buttons down the front of their uniforms, red caps on their heads with a round button right in front. As they came closer I saw them playing flashy, shiny instruments that bounced the bright sunshine right in my eyes. Horns all raised up high, blasting so very loud. Some long ones [trombones] sliding in and out. Big fat ones going Umph, Umph. Banjos played fast, drums rat-a-tatting, and a huge round drum that boomed-boomed as it went by. [8]

Scott Joplin composed ragtime's most famous piece, "Maple Leaf Rag."

Musicians in the marching bands often improvised solos to play above the written music. And many of the musicians also played in other bands, performing ragtime, blues, or other styles. As they traveled from one musical setting to the other, they began mixing the many musical styles to form a completely new musical genre.

Buddy Bolden's Blues

No one knows for certain the name of the person who first synthesized ragtime, blues, field hollers, and marching

Brass Bands

In Jazz: The First Century, *edited by John Edward Hasse, jazz musician Michael White describes brass bands as they appeared during the early twentieth century:*

Boom! . . . Boom! . . . Boom! Those first thunderous blasts from the big bass drum signal the start of a musically led passage deep into the soul of New Orleans. Whenever the context of the drum call and improvised brass-band music that follow . . . everyone is welcome to participate in the spirited—and often spiritual—occasion.

One, two, even three ten-piece brass bands—each member wearing a uniform and band cap—may line up for the procession. Each group might have three trumpets to improvise melodies, two trombones to slide and growl, a clarinet to sing and dance above the ensemble, and two saxophones to lay down powerful riffs. The foundation is a swinging rhythm section with a lightly rapping snare drum, a roaring bass drum to pour out endless synco-pated rhythms, and a whopping tuba to anchor everything with bass lines. Whether jazzing up a standard religious hymn, a traditional march, a popular song, a rag, or a blues, the band struts along and marks the time in easy, neither-too-fast-nor-too-slow dance tempos.

Each band is led by an elegantly dressed grand marshal, who waves his handkerchief and carries a decorated umbrella as he gracefully dances along. . . . Club divisions attempt to outdo each other in dance and dress. . . .

As the parade proceeds, it collects an endless number of "second liners"—hundreds of anonymous onlookers who follow and dance alongside the parade. . . . Standard music rules are broken, twisted, and stretched in favor of fresh creative expression that matches the wild passion of the dances. . . . As the dancing and music reach ever-higher levels of intensity, the participants may feel they're losing themselves in a swirling sea of people, motion, heat, scents, and sounds.

music into jazz, but the credit is often given to bandleader Charles "Buddy" Bolden, who was born in 1877. Bolden played the cornet, a three-valved brass instrument that resembles a shortened trumpet but has a softer, warmer sound.

Bolden was a New Orleans legend in his own time, as pianist Jelly Roll Morton describes him: "He drank all the whiskey he could find, never wore a collar and tie, had his shirt busted open so all the girls [could] see that red flannel undershirt, always having a ball—Buddy Bolden was the most powerful [cornetist] in history."[9]

As early as 1901 Bolden was improvising cornet licks in front of a group composed of a clarinetist, trombonist, guitarist, bassist, and drummer (a musical configuration of players that later became standard in jazz groups). Bolden played in bars and dance halls throughout greater New Orleans, and he was often seen on Sundays in the city's Johnson Park playing to large audiences. Although no known recording of Bolden exists, he left behind songs such as "If You Don't Shake, You Don't Get No Cake" and "Funky Butt," which became early jazz standards. But Bolden's music was based on the rousing spirituals he had heard in church. As John Edward Hasse writes in *Jazz: The First Century,* "Bolden is said to have been inspired by music of 'holy roller' church, and he delivered sound in many forms, from rough and loud to slow and low-down."[10]

Bolden's behavior was as wild as his music, and in 1907 he suffered a mental breakdown at the age of twenty-nine. He was diagnosed with dementia and confined to the Louisiana State Asylum, where he died in 1931. Still, his contribution to jazz is unquestioned. In *A New History of Jazz,* Alyn Shipton lists Bolden's musical accomplishments:

[Famous] for his sheer volume, Bolden played largely by ear and was credited by many of those who heard him as being the first to bring the explicitly African qualities of flattened blue notes, vocalized tones, and "hot" syncopation into the ragtime setting—in other words, he was seen as the progenitor of improvisation in jazz.[11]

After Bolden

Nobody knows, of course, what other contributions Bolden might have been capable of making, but other musicians acted as innovators who established and expanded the new art form. In 1907, for example, Joe Oliver started playing with brass bands and was soon known as "the Cornet King." Oliver was the first to use rubber cups, derby hats, and other objects, known as mutes, to cover the bell of his horn. This innovation allowed King Oliver, and later millions of other horn players, to create special effects such as the "wa-wa" that imitated, in an exaggerated way, the sound of the human voice.

Other musicians saw to it that jazz spread beyond its original base in and around New Orleans. Trombonist Edward "Kid" Ory was another jazz original and the first to take jazz music west when he moved to Los Angeles in 1914 and formed Kid Ory's Original Creole Band. Ory was famous for his loud, ragged style, known as tailgate, and in 1922 he and his band members became the first African Americans from New Orleans to record their music.

Cornet player Freddie Keppard played with Ory, and his creative sounds helped make the Original Creole Band very popular. As pianist Jelly Roll Morton once said, "There was no

Kid Ory introduced jazz to the west coast when he moved to Los Angeles and formed Kid Ory's Original Creole Band.

end to his ideas. . . . He could play a chorus eight or ten different ways." [12] One story often repeated about Keppard says that he was offered the chance to make the first jazz record by the Victor Talking Machine Company, but he turned it down because he was afraid that someone would hear the record and steal his licks.

The Original Creole Band toured the United States continually, playing for white audiences in vaudeville theaters and introducing new audiences to the New Orleans sound. While Keppard and Ory introduced jazz to a wider audience in America, Sidney Bechet, a wizard on the clarinet, brought jazz to the attention of the world. Bechet began working with some of New Orleans's most renowned brass bands in 1910, when he was only thirteen years old. In 1917 he hit the road, touring the United States in bands playing the soprano saxophone (an instrument modeled on the clarinet but made of brass). In 1919 Bechet became one of the first jazz players to tour Europe, and his playing was praised by the highly respected Swiss conductor Ernest Ansermet, who said Bechet was "an extraordinary clarinet virtuoso . . . and artist of genius [who played jazz songs] equally admirable for their richness of invention, force of accent, and daring in novelty and the unexpected." [13]

Jelly Roll Morton

What Bechet was to the sax, Jelly Roll Morton, born Ferdinand Joseph

As one of the first jazz players to tour Europe, clarinetist Sidney Bechet is credited with bringing jazz to the attention of the world.

LaMothe, was to piano. Morton, who worked nightly in the Storyville brothels, transformed the somewhat rigid structure of music for ragtime piano into the free-flowing sounds of jazz, improvising riffs, embellishing melodies with cascades of notes, and swinging the bass rhythm with his left hand. Morton loved to boast that he had single-handedly invented jazz. Although this claim was hotly disputed by others, Morton is the first person to write his jazz compositions down on sheet music. This allowed other musi-

cians across the globe to learn real jazz firsthand from Morton's notes written on the page.

Morton was the offspring of light-skinned Creoles, and his light complexion meant that he could be hired in Storyville brothels where darker-skinned African Americans were not welcome. The pianist continued to face prejudice, however, as Louis Armstrong later wrote:

Jelly Roll with lighter skin than the average piano players got the

The Original Dixieland Jazz Band was one of the first white bands to capitalize on the jazz craze that was sweeping the nation.

job because they did not want a Black piano player for the job. He claimed he was from an Indian or Spanish race. No Cullud [colored] at all. He was a big Bragadossa [braggart]. Lots of big talk. . . . Jelly Roll made so much money in tips he had a diamond inserted in one of his teeth. No matter how much his diamond sparkled he still had to eat in the kitchen, the same as we Blacks.[14]

Jazz Goes on Record

By the mid-1910s jazz musicians from New Orleans were traveling across America playing for large, appreciative audiences, and before long, white bands got into the act. The Original Dixieland Jazz Band, made up of white players and led by Italian American cornetist Nick La Rocca, profited by this trend. Curiously, this New Orleans–based Dixieland group had never heard the term *jazz* until they played Chicago in 1916. As La Rocca told one interviewer, "We only called the music 'jazz' after someone in the audience one night in Chicago kept hollering at us to "Jazz it up!", and it seemed to fit our music. No, I never heard the word in New Orleans. I found out later it was a [curse] word in Chicago, but I guess we purified it." [15]

The Original Dixieland Jazz Band (ODJB) moved on to New York City in 1917, landing a gig at the prestigious Reisenweber's Restaurant. At first the crowds were hostile towards the musicians because they were unable to understand their swinging, ragtime sound. Within a few weeks, however, people began to appreciate the music for its danceable beat and the band became a sensation, drawing huge crowds. As the lines of patrons waiting in front of Reisenweber's began to stretch around the block, the ODJB was hired to perform for the following eighteen months.

Spotting a profitable trend, Victor Record executives ushered the group into the recording studio, and the ODJB became the first jazz band to make a record. When "Livery Stable Blues" was released in March 1917, it sold 250,000 copies within months. At that time no other record—classical, opera, marching band, or any other style—had ever sold such an astonishing number. "Livery Stable Blues" would eventually sell millions of copies throughout the world, and the sound pioneered by poor black musicians in New Orleans would be heard from Los Angeles to London.

Some critics found the music of the ODJB extremely comical: They played fast and furious with the drummer pounding out a heavy beat while the cornet and clarinet improvised on the high notes and the saxophones and trombone looped through running bass and melody lines. Added to the fact that they played fast to begin with, the normally four- or five-minute-long songs were sped up in order to fit them onto 78 rpm records, which provided less than three minutes playing time per side. This turned the ragtime jazz into a musical version of the slapstick comedy seen in popular movies by Charlie Chaplin and Buster Keaton. And the hilarity was heightened at a break in the "Livery Stable Blues" where the cornet imitates the sound of horse whinny, the clarinet in response sounds like a crowing rooster, and the trombone rips out the low-down sound of a braying donkey.

Although the public snapped up the records of the ODJB, critics panned the music, calling it crude and harsh. One unnamed critic in New York's *Sunday Sun* wrote, "The musical riot that breaks forth from clarinet, trombone, cornet, piano, drums and variants of [other] instruments resembles nothing so much as a chorus of hunting hounds on the scent [of a fox] with an occasional explosion in the subway thrown in for good measure." [16]

The music also found critics within the African American jazz community who felt that the white version of jazz was "cleaned up" and was less authentic than the music invented by black

The Jazz Drum Set

Jazz has always been rhythm based, and early bands often had two drummers. The first played a snare drum, a round drum with a strand of wire stretched across the bottom head. When struck on top, the snare gives a sustained rattle, or "sizzle" sound. The other drummer played a big bass drum and cymbal.

In the beginning most jazz drummers could not afford fancy equipment and were often forced to improvise drum sets. These players put together a "kit" consisting of a snare drum, several small bass drums called tom-toms, and a few cymbals. Mickey Hart describes this process in *Drumming at the Edge of Magic,* writing, "drummers began ransacking the percussive inventory . . . [taking] elements from all over the planet— snares and bass drums from Europe, the tom-tom from China, cymbals from Turkey—and along with such homely additions as cowbells, anvils, and woodblocks invented a new kind of drumming and, incidentally, a new instrument."

The drum kit was again transformed around 1920, when jazz drummer Warren "Baby" Dodds added a bass drum that could be struck with a foot pedal, a concept now universally accepted by drummers across the globe. At that time,

Zildjian, a Turkish cymbal maker who had been in business for almost five hundred years, began selling its instruments throughout the United States. Drummers could now easily purchase what are known as crash cymbals and sizzle cymbals (for their tones) and ride cymbals (for the way they are continually tapped, or ridden). Finally, innovative drummer Vic Berton added two small cymbals, about thirteen inches across, to a pedal-operated stand, or "high hat," and the modern drum kit was complete. Today, nearly every style of popular music relies on a drummer playing a drum kit, an instrument that might not exist without the clever invention of jazz drummers in New Orleans at the turn of the twentieth century.

Warren "Baby" Dodds revolutionized the drum kit by introducing a bass drum that could be struck by means of a foot pedal.

musicians. It was hard to argue with success, however, and the ODJB introduced jazz to a huge audience. In addition, the band inspired a new generation of musicians across the globe to learn to play jazz.

A New Era in Music

By 1919 the efforts of Bolden, Oliver, Ory, and the ODJB had ushered in a new era in music. The musicians had differentiated their new art form from ragtime, blues, and marching music in several important ways: The majority of the music was improvised, and when five or seven players jammed together, the music got wilder and more complex. In addition, the rhythm was syncopated to give the music swing. And the band leaders wrote much of their own music as opposed to following scores by professional composers.

Jazz music was now heard live and on records in Chicago, New York, and Europe as well as in New Orleans. The music that was once confined to the sordid brothels of the Big Easy found new respectability in restaurants, theaters, and concert halls. At the dawn of the Roaring Twenties, jazz music was poised to take the world by storm.

Chapter Two

The Swingin' Jazz Age

In 1920, at the beginning of the era known as the Jazz Age, many of New Orleans's top players headed north to Chicago, where they were discovered by both black and white audiences. The move away from the Big Easy was motivated by the fact that the legendary brothels of Storyville were shut down by New Orleans's city officials in 1917, throwing hundreds of musicians out of work. These people were attracted to Chicago not only because it was a growing and prosperous city but also because it was at the center of the U.S. recording industry at that time. With its burgeoning nightclub scene, the Windy City beckoned to many of New Orleans's most celebrated jazz players, including Sidney Bechet, Joe "King" Oliver, Jelly Roll Morton, and others.

As Chicago became the center of the jazz world, several types of bands emerged. Foremost was the all-star band, such as King Oliver's Creole Jazz Band. Next were the white bands from New Orleans, such as the New Orleans Rhythm Kings. Finally, there were the bands of local Chicago musicians who imitated the sounds of the New Orleans groups. Some of these musicians, such as Benny Goodman, Gene Krupa, and Jack Teagarden, would become jazz superstars during the 1930s.

With so many musicians flooding into one town, only the best performers were able to rise above the crowd. These top instrumentalists were able to differentiate themselves by playing the most unusual solos and the fastest riffs. As a result, the 1920s emerged as the era of the solo player, led by one of the greatest musicians in jazz history, Louis Armstrong, whose tone, musical range, and command of the trumpet surpassed all others. While earlier jazz had been roughly based on ragtime, blues, and marching music, with the emergence of the star soloist, the music took on a new complexity.

Whereas earlier jazz music had been confined to short, improvisational pieces, the new works were longer and freer. And in this atmosphere of experimentation, jazz musicians discovered new sounds on their instruments and combined instruments in unique ways. As Jazz producer and critic Michael Brooks writes in *Jazz: The First Century,* "[What made the musicians'] accomplishments all the more remarkable was the fact that they did it in the restrictive sphere of popular entertainment, where the first order of business was to keep the crowds coming."[17]

The Roaring Twenties

The new, hot sounds of jazz incubated during an exceptional set of social conditions that were unique in American history and led to the 1920s being labeled the Jazz Age. The automobile, a relatively new invention, offered people real freedom and mobility for the first time. Meanwhile, the American economy was growing at its fastest rate ever. Fueled by easy credit, the stock market soared as even people of modest means invested, and a new class of millionaires was minted virtually overnight.

At the same time, electric lighting and refrigeration were not only becoming widely available but also affordable, and they quickly changed America. By the end of the decade nearly every home in the United States contained at least one radio, which had first come onto the scene after World War I. As millions of homes and businesses were wired for power, the sales of new, improved electric phonographs soared,

Chicago, Illinois

Wisconsin

Michigan

New York

Chicago

Pennsylvania

Illinois

Ohio

Indiana

West Virginia

Kentucky

Virginia

Why Chicago?

There were several reasons why the jazz scene shifted to Chicago during the 1920s. The first was the move by African Americans away from the agricultural southern states to the industrial North. Known as the Great Migration, this trend saw over fifty thousand blacks moving to Chicago between 1915 and 1920. These people were fleeing the poverty and prejudice of the South and hoping to improve their lives by working in the Windy City's steel mills, slaughter houses, and factories. And they brought with them their knowledge of jazz, blues, and ragtime music.

The passage of the Eighteenth Amendment to the Constitution and the Volstead Act, which banned the manufacture and sale of alcohol and gave federal agencies the authority to enforce the ban, also contributed to Chicago's rise to prominence. The amendment, known as Prohibition, turned millions of otherwise law-abiding citizens who continued to drink into criminals. Soon, real criminals took advantage of the opportunity to make money. With its central Midwest location, Chicago quickly became the major hub for gangsters, illegal nightclubs called speakeasies, and the illegal liquor trade. Much like the seamy brothels of Storyville, which had employed jazz players in earlier years, the speakeasies were a magnet for musicians. While white gangsters were fighting bloody turf wars in the streets, they were also hiring hundreds of black musicians to play at the thousands of speakeasies they controlled throughout the region. For the average American these clubs provided a thrilling way to break the law by simply drinking a martini. For jazz musicians, this opportunity led to a golden age of innovation.

making jazz—and other types of music—available to millions of people for the first time. In addition, advances in recording technology allowed an immense improvement in phonograph records. Musical subtleties that had previously been lost during the recording process could now be heard, inspiring jazz composers to write still more complex and dynamic arrangements.

Overshadowing all of these changes, the federal government was enforcing a law known as Prohibition, passed in 1919, which made the manufacture and distribution of all alcoholic beverages illegal in the United States. Banning alcohol did not end demand for it, however. As the price of an illicit drink soared from twenty-five cents to two dollars, thousands of illegal nightclubs and cabarets, called speakeasies, opened practically overnight. Those who ran the speakeasies hired black jazz musicians to attract adventurous young white people, who spent freely and danced to suggestive new dances named the Black Bottom and the Charleston.

Parents fumed that jazz was ruining the country, but young people streamed into the clubs. And jazz, in word and music, was everywhere. Fashionable clothes were called jazz dresses, modern syncopated verse was called jazz poetry, and fast old cars were called jazzy jalopies.

As well-to-do white patrons and black musicians rubbed elbows in the speakeasies, it became fashionable to support this aspect of African American culture. Jazz, blues, and ragtime records by black artists, called race records, were purchased in great numbers by

Chicago's Michigan Avenue in the 1920s. During Prohibition, the city was a mecca for those seeking illegal alcohol and jazzy nightclubs.

white people. In Chicago, New York City, and elsewhere, plays, revues, and theatrical productions with all-black casts were packing in white audiences. It was an unprecedented meeting of the races, with jazz music at its center. As critic J.A. Rogers wrote in *Survey* magazine in 1925,

> Jazz has come to stay because it is an expression of the times, of the breathless, energetic, superactive times in which we are living. . . . The Negro musicians of America are playing a great part in this change. They have an open mind, and unbiassed outlook. They are not hampered by conventions or traditions, and with their new ideas, their constant experiment, they are causing new blood to flow in the veins of music. The jazz players make their instruments do entirely new things, things finished musicians are taught to avoid. They are pathfinders into new realms. [18]

Armstrong Comes to Town

While these astonishing changes were taking place, jazz music continued to chart its own course through the speakeasies, ballrooms, and dance halls of Chicago. And jazz historians can pinpoint the exact date that the music changed forever.

On August 8, 1922, cornet player Louis Armstrong stepped off the train in downtown Chicago. He carried with him only his battered horn and a

Legendary jazz trumpeter Louis Armstrong plays at the Savoy Hotel in London.

threadbare tuxedo that he wore for his performances. Although he was poor, Armstrong had something money could not buy—a phenomenal tone, a gift for improvisation, and the ability to blow his horn in an upper register out of the reach of other trumpeters.

Armstrong had been invited to the Windy City by King Oliver, who had been nurturing the young musician for years in New Orleans. Oliver's influence on Armstrong is described by Richard Hadlock in *Jazz Masters of the 20's:* "Louis picked up valuable secrets of rhythmic phrasing, of good blues playing, and of establishing a sure, driving lead melody line." [19]

Armstrong was born in New Orleans in 1901 in a neighborhood so rough that it was known as "the Battlefield." He grew up extremely poor and hungry and was placed in a juvenile detention center called the Colored Waif's Home after being arrested at the age of eleven for shooting a gun into the air on New Year's Eve.

Louis had been playing a battered trumpet he had picked up for five dollars, and when he went into the Colored Waif's Home, he was quickly acknowledged as the best horn player in the marching band. The first time the band paraded through Storyville with Armstrong at the lead, listeners on balconies and sidewalks rewarded their incredible sound with such generous tips that the school had enough money to buy all new instruments for the band.

After he was released in 1913, Armstrong began playing the toughest brothels in Storyville, where his loud, clear improvisations became legend. Because his cheeks puffed out so far when he blew his horn, he was given many nicknames, including Gatemouth, Rhythm Jaws, Dippermouth, and Satchelmouth. The last name, pronounced *Satchmo,* stuck, and Armstrong would be referred to by that name for the rest of his life.

After arriving in Chicago, Armstrong spent two momentous years playing with Oliver's Creole Jazz Band. From the very beginning, Satchmo had the uncanny ability to complement Oliver's improvisations so closely that their music sounded as though they were playing from scores that had already been written down. Whatever riff or line Oliver would invent, Armstrong could play in harmony a quarter beat behind. Other times, the two would trade licks and try to outplay, or "cut," each other on stage.

The Creoles played in the flourishing black neighborhood on Chicago's South Side where a nine-block stretch of South State Street, known as the Stroll, rivaled New York's Broadway for its number of clubs and theaters. One bedazzled musician described it, saying there "was so much music in the air . . . an instrument held outside at midnight would play itself." [20]

Black jazz fans flocked to a nightclub called Lincoln Gardens in order to hear the Creole Jazz Band. The group featured Johnny Dodds on clarinet, his brother "Baby" Dodds on drums, Honoré Dutrey on trombone, Bill Johnson on banjo and bass, and Lil Hardin on piano. But, most of all, people wanted to hear Oliver and Armstrong trading cornet solos, playing riffs in unison, and creating the most danceable beat on the street. As word spread about the talents of Armstrong, white people came to the club eager to dance. Baby Dodds recalls, "One couldn't help but dance to that band. The music was so wonderful that [patrons] had to do something, even if there was only room to bounce around. . . . We didn't choose any one number to play well. We had the sort of band that, when we played a number, we put all our hearts into it." [21]

Satchmo Goes on Record

In April 1923 the Creole Jazz Band went into the studio to cut its first records. Although the music recorded at these sessions reflected the traditional sound of a New Orleans ensemble band, there was one important difference, according to Brooks: "[The] interplay between Oliver and Armstrong drove listeners wild, making them more aware of individual instruments."[22]

When the records were released, songs such as "Dippermouth Blues" jumped off

The Amazing Lil Armstrong

Although Louis Armstrong is renowned for the incredible jazz records he made with his Hot Five and Hot Seven bands, what is less well known is that several of the greatest songs on those records were written and arranged by his wife Lil Armstrong. The following biography is from the Lil Hardin-Armstrong website:

Lil Hardin-Armstrong was the most prominent woman in early jazz. She played piano, composed, and arranged for most of the important Hot Bands from New Orleans. While working at a music store in Chicago, she was invited to play with Sugar Johnny's Creole Orchestra, from there she went to Freddie Keppard's Original Creole Orchestra, and then led her own band at the Dreamland Café . . . in Chicago. In 1921 she joined King Oliver's Creole Jazz Band where she meet Louis Armstrong. They were married in 1924.

Lil was Louis Armstrong's second wife and she is generally credited with persuading Louis to be more ambitious, and leave King Oliver's Creole Jazz Band. Lil was a major contributor to Louis Armstrong's Hot Five and Hot Seven recordings. She played piano and sang occasionally, and composed several of the group's major songs, including "Struttin' with Some Barbecue." Lil was the leader of several other recording groups, including Lil's Hot Shots and the New Orleans Wanderers. She and Louis were separated in 1931 and were divorced in 1938, although they remained friends for life. In the late 1930s Lil recast herself as a Swing vocalist and cut 26 vocal sides for Decca records. . . . She continued to record sporadically up until 1963. . . . Strangely enough, Lil died while taking part in a Louis Armstrong Memorial Concert in Chicago while playing "St. Louis Blues," just two months after Louis had died.

The Hot Five was a famed jazz band whose members included (from left) Louis Armstrong, Johnny St. Cyr, Johnny Dodds, Kid Ory, and Armstrong's wife, Lil.

the shelves in record stores. And for the first time, the record-buying public got to hear Oliver's and Armstrong's dueling cornets in "Jazzin' Babies' Blues," "Snake Rag," and others. These records garnered a huge audience for Armstrong throughout North America and Europe.

Armstrong's career was boosted further when, in 1924, he married Lil Hardin, a pianist, singer, composer, and arranger who also played with King Oliver. The ambitious Mrs. Armstrong encouraged her husband to leave Oliver's band and head for the big time in New York City, where he played a thirteen-month stint with Fletcher Hendersen's Orchestra. During this time Armstrong sat in on a recording session with the legendary blues singer Bessie Smith. Her recording of "St. Louis Blues," made with Satchmo blowing the blues between vocal lines, is still considered a classic.

Musical Firsts

Armstrong, however, did not confine himself to playing the cornet. After his New York engagements, Armstrong moved back to Chicago to play with Lil's band at the Dreamland Café, where he perfected the raspy singing style that would later become his trademark.

Between November 1925 and December 1928 Satchmo put together several bands, known as the Hot Five and the Hot Seven, that only played for recording sessions. The resulting records became some of the most influential sides in jazz history. With Armstrong taking extended solos—and allowing the other musicians the same courtesy—the era of the ensemble jazz band quickly faded, replaced by the sound of the virtuoso solo performer. On "Gut Bucket Blues," Armstrong even introduces each player by name as they take a solo, a first in recording history.

Another jazz first, for which Armstrong deserves credit, was the result of a happy accident. During the 1926 recording of "Heebie Jeebies," Armstrong accidentally dropped his lyric sheet on the floor. Rather than stop the music, the record producer motioned for Satchmo to make up some words. Armstrong improvised a string of nonsensical syllables with vocal growls and rumbles meant to sound like a deeply soulful trumpet solo. This was the first recording of the technique known as scat singing, and when the record was released, scat became one of the hottest styles among jazz singers.

Armstrong's Hot Band records highlight Satchmo at the height of his creative peak. Alyn Shipton describes the importance of the records:

> The discs . . . confirmed that Armstrong had successfully combined emotional depth, rhythmic innovation, and a liberating sense of solo freedom into a heady and original mixture. He pushed at the boundaries of the cornet's range. Even in his hottest solos, he ex-

plored a lyricism that might, in part, have come from his love for light classics and opera. . . . Overall, he brought a new set of [creative] qualities into jazz, a sense that there could be considerable artistic worth in music conceived as popular entertainment. [23]

Developing the Chicago Sound

When not recording, Armstrong played to mostly black audiences on Chicago's South Side. But as early as 1923, when Satchmo was still playing with King Oliver, a group of teenaged white boys had begun showing up at his performances. These young men were from an upper-class West Side Chicago neighborhood known as Austin, and all attended Austin High School.

Members of what became known as the Austin High Gang included clarinetists Benny Goodman and Pee Wee Russell, horn player and singer Jack Teagarden, drummer David Tough, saxophone player Bud Freeman, and guitarist Eddie Condon. The group of boys, many of whom were in the school band, first heard jazz on phonograph records in a neighborhood ice cream parlor. After wearing out the grooves on several records by the New Orleans Rhythm Kings, the boys, some still too young to drive, journeyed down to the South Side on their bicycles to hear live jazz.

At first, the patrons of the club were hostile to the upper-class white schoolboys. But Oliver, who always believed in helping young musicians, nodded to them from the stage, and the crowd accepted the young outsiders in their midst. In *Jazz: A Film by Ken Burns,* trumpeter Wynton Marsalis describes the scene:

> Now . . . when these white kids come . . . to hear King Oliver and Louis Armstrong playing this music, we have to realize that this is some of the most abstract and sophisticated music that anybody has ever heard, short of Bach. And . . . they're attracted to the groove and the feeling of the music . . . and they're saying, "Man, this is what we want to play like." They start playing, and they keep coming down. And they start learning . . . and the bandleader, the great Joe Oliver, from New Orleans . . . says, "Let these white kids come in and listen to this music," not because he wanted to patronize them. Because . . . he knew that they were really listening to this music. [24]

After hearing Oliver's band night after night, the Austin High Gang began to develop a style of their own. After graduating from high school, the group began playing engagements around Chicago,

King Oliver's Creole Jazz Band plays in a bar in Chicago. Their music inspired a group of white high school students, known as the Austin High Gang, to develop a jazz style of their own.

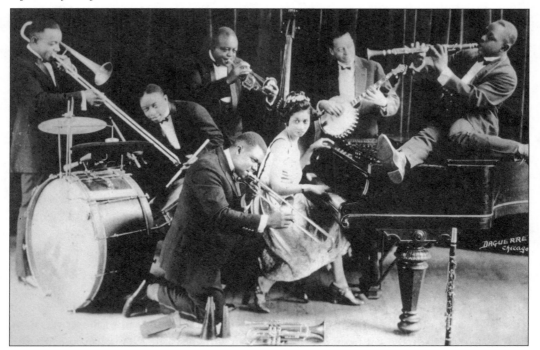

blending New Orleans jazz and an aggressive, northern beat more reminiscent of the *rat-tat-tat* of a machine gun. This sound was distinctive and soon became known as the Chicago style.

Inspired by the Austin High Gang's example, black and white musicians began jamming together. Although the whites were free to journey to the South Side to listen to black jazz artists, blacks were banned from Chicago's downtown clubs. But the musicians had mutual respect for each other, and after the clubs closed, the white musicians would journey to the South Side to jam with the African Americans. These sessions were called breakfast dances because they continued past five o'clock in the morning. And along the way, the academic musical-school background of the whites and the creative impulses of the blacks became intertwined into the Chicago sound.

The Stride Piano

Although Chicago remained an important center for jazz during the 1920s, New York City—a town jazz musicians had named "the Big Apple"—was a worthy rival. By 1920 the city had more African American residents than any other, including Chicago, and most lived in the vibrant Harlem neighborhood. In fact, the neighborhood was at the center of a growing creative movement among black poets, painters, authors, historians, and playwrights known as the Harlem Renaissance.

New York jazz had a unique sound thanks to the pianists who were the kings of Harlem jazz. These musicians played "stride piano," an engaging style with roots in ragtime. Stride players use their left hand to play percussive, "striding" midrange chords and bass notes, while their right hand "tickles" out the melody on the upper keys. The sound was so large and powerful that it could be described as orchestral, or sounding like a full orchestra.

Few piano players possessed the technical and creative mastery necessary for playing stride. But New Jersey–born pianist James P. Johnson took the style, which had been pioneered by Jelly Roll Morton during the 1910s, and made it his own. Johnson earned the title "the Father of Stride Piano" because, as Gridley writes, "Johnson dispensed with the stiff rhythms . . . and march-like bass of ragtime, while contributing a fluidity, a harmonic sophistication and an attention to chord voicings. He perfected the orchestral approach to jazz piano playing, as though he were a one-man band." [25]

In addition to his influential playing style, Johnson was a popular—and prolific—composer who wrote 230 songs, 19 symphonic works, and 11 musicals. But his most famous composition was "The Charleston," which had an accompanying dance. This song brought jazz to a wide audience and became synonymous with the Jazz Age.

Duke Ellington's Toodle-Oo

Johnson often participated in cutting contests with other notable stride players such as Willie "the Lion" Smith and

Bix Beiderbecke

Before Louis Armstrong moved to Chicago, he played on riverboats that steamed up and down the Mississippi River. In 1919 a young white trumpet player from Davenport, Iowa, named Leon "Bix" Beiderbecke heard Satchmo's cornet blasting from a passing riverboat. This inspired him to begin a career in jazz music. Beiderbecke's short life is described by the Leon "Bix" Beiderbecke website:

Bix Beiderbecke was one of the great jazz musicians of the 1920's, he was also a child of the Jazz Age who drank himself to an early grave with illegal Prohibition liquor. His hard drinking and beautiful tone on the cornet made him a legend among musicians during his life. The legend of Bix grew even larger after he died. Bix never learned to read music very well, but he had an amazing ear even as a child. . . . In 1923 Beiderbecke joined the Wolverine Orchestra and recorded with them the following year. . . . In 1926 he spent some time with Frankie Trumbauer's Orchestra where he recorded his solo piano master-piece "In a Mist." He also recorded some of his best work with Trumbauer and guitarist, Eddie Lang, under the name of Tram, Bix, and Eddie. Bix was able to bone up on his sight reading enough to . . . [sign] up as a soloist with Paul Whiteman's Orchestra. Whiteman's Orchestra was the most popular band of the 1920's and Bix enjoyed the prestige and money of playing with such a successful outfit, but it didn't stop his drinking. In 1929 Bix's drinking began to catch up with him. He suffered from delirium tremens [delirium and tremors caused by prolonged and excessive alcohol abuse] and he had a nervous breakdown while playing with the Paul Whiteman Orchestra, and was eventually sent back to his parents in Davenport, Iowa to recover. . . . He returned to New York in 1930 . . . and holed himself up in a rooming house in Queens, New York where he drank a lot and worked on his beautiful solo piano pieces "Candlelight," "Flashes," and "In The Dark." He died at age 28 in 1931 during an alcoholic seizure.

others. These events, in which pianists attempted to outplay each other with nearly impossible riffs and runs, attracted many young musicians, including an up-and-coming pianist named Edward "Duke" Ellington, who was awed by Johnson's creative licks, fast hands, and precision runs.

Ellington was born in 1899 and was raised in middle-class comfort in Washington, D.C. He moved to Harlem in 1923, and by the mid-1920s he had formed his own red-hot band, the Washingtonians, which combined the ragtime jazz Ellington recalled from his youth with stride piano and Armstrong's New Orleans–style improvisations.

Trumpet player Bubber Miley gave the Washingtonians a unique voice when he used his mute to obtain a down-and-dirty, blues-drenched, "gut bucket" effect that Ellington called the jungle sound. The recording of "East St. Louis Toodle-Oo" is a good example of this jazz strain. Describing it, Ellington said that Miley was "the body and soul of Soulville. He was raised on soul and saturated and marinated in soul. Every note he played was soul." [26]

By 1927 Ellington was pioneering a new type of jazz, composing music that mixed jazz with the lush orchestral sounds heard in popular music and theatrical musicals. By using strings,

The Cotton Club was an exclusive bar and restaurant located in Harlem that employed black performers to entertain the all-white crowd.

In addition to playing for the Cotton Club, Duke Ellington (left) and his band made 150 records between 1927 and 1931.

brass, and woodwinds, Ellington forged a sound all his own. Critics responded positively and began to call Ellington's music sophisticated.

Ellington's big break came in 1927, when his group became the house band for the Cotton Club. Although it was located in Harlem, the expensive club, which was decorated in the style of a nineteenth-century southern mansion, catered only to white people. All the waiters and waitresses were black, as were the dancers, singers, comedians, and other entertainers who appeared alongside Ellington. The club's music, plantation theme, and raucous dance pieces provided wealthy white people a chance to experience what they thought of as a "primitive 'African' or 'jungle' atmosphere,"[27] according to Shipton.

The ten-piece band, now renamed Duke Ellington and His Cotton Club Orchestra, quickly achieved national fame when its performances were featured in radio broadcasts made from the club every Saturday night. With his newfound fame and money, Ellington was able to hire the best musicians in New York—and he wrote stunning arrangements that allowed them to showcase their talents.

Ellington played Harlem's Cotton Club off and on until 1933. And between 1927 and 1931 his orchestra made 150 records in 64 different recording sessions. When not playing and recording in New York, Ellington toured extensively in the United States and Europe. Wherever he played, his manager, Irving Mills, sent out press releases that read, "Come on! Get hot! Get happy! [With] Harlems' jazz king, blaring, crooning, burning up the stage with his red hot rhythms, moaning saxophones, wailing cornets, laughing trombones, [and] screaming clarinets." [28] During his West Coast tours, Ellington also began appearing in Hollywood movies beginning in 1929 with *Black and Tan Fantasy,* named after one of his famous songs.

Ellington's many memorable compositions, such as "Mood Indigo," "Sophisticated Lady," and "Take the 'A' Train" utilized catchy and unusual melodies that bridged the gap between 1920s jazz combos and the big-band era of the 1930s. Since they introduced the world to the strutting, swinging sounds of Ellington's New York, they have become jazz classics across the globe. Duke Ellington remained an influential force in jazz, and even after his death from cancer in 1974, his music never really went out of style.

And thanks to Ellington and Armstrong, the 1920s would always be remembered as a time when New Orleans–style jazz grew up, gained influence and sophistication, moved to Chicago, New York, and beyond, and changed the musical landscape forever.

Chapter Three

Dancing to Swing

Whereas the 1920s earned the nickname "the Jazz Age," the period between 1930 and the 1940s is known as the swing era. Ironically, this was also a decade during which the nation endured an economic downturn known as the Great Depression. Despite the harsh economic times, however, people went out and danced to jazz as never before.

In an era when large families often were crammed into small apartments, dance halls offered young people an escape from the harsh realities of daily life. For fifty cents on a weeknight and seventy-five cents on a weekend, courting couples could swing and sway the night away to the big-band music of Benny Goodman, Glenn Miller, Tommy Dorsey, Artie Shaw, Ella Fitzgerald, and many others.

Swing music was an extension of the New Orleans–style jazz that was almost single-handedly invented by Louis Armstrong. Satchmo was famous for swinging the rhythm of jazz by playing slightly ahead of the beat. As he gained national popularity in the first half of the 1930s, he inspired other musicians to do the same.

At the same time, players from across the musical spectrum began playing swing as it became the most popular music in America. Accordingly, the overall sophistication of the music increased. In addition, these talented musicians, many of them classically trained, played tighter, faster, and with greater agility.

One way that swing music differed from the jazz of the 1920s was that swing bands utilized twelve to twenty musicians rather than the five- or seven-piece combos that had been the rule earlier. These big bands added instruments not commonly heard before in jazz, such as saxophones, high-hat cymbals, guitars instead of banjos, and string basses instead of tubas. In *Jazz: A Film by Ken Burns,* music critic Gary Giddens describes how big-band instruments were arranged:

Big bands such as the Glenn Miller orchestra used instruments not commonly heard before in jazz, like saxophones and string basses.

Basically you have four sections in a big band. You've got the saxophone section, the reed section, which often has clarinets. You have the trumpet section and the trombone section which became more important as the years went by. Originally there usually would just be one trombone. And the trombones and the trumpets together are the brasses. And then you have the rhythm section which was . . . just drums, bass and piano. And these sections work like gears in a machinery. They interlock and what the orchestrator [arranger] has to do is to find really exciting, inventive ways to blend these instruments, to work one section against another and to create a new music with instrumentation that is again, purely American. It's an American invention. It's what we have instead of the symphony.[29]

Swing bands, relying more on written arrangements, placed greater emphasis on and utilized the power of solo improvisation rather than group jams. Big bands featured performers and conductors such as clarinetist Benny Goodman, pianist William "Count" Basie, and saxophonists Coleman Hawkins and Lester Young. The music these individuals produced was so distinctive that their names have become synonymous with 1930s swing music.

Swing bands also featured vocalists who could sing written arrangements or scat improvised melodies. The status of the singer changed, however, over the course of the swing era. During the 1930s bands and their conductors were the main attractions at the ballrooms. In fact, singers were called standup vocalists because they would sit in a chair by the side of the stage and only appeared front and center when they would stand up and sing a song or two. But singers

A National Obsession

In Jazz: The First Century, *John Edward Hasse writes about the cultural phenomena surrounding swing music during the 1930s:*

Public dancing became, by the 1930s, one of the key American courtship rituals. For many young people, swing music and dancing served as important emotional outlets; for others, they offered much-needed escape from the economic difficulties of the lingering Depression. With partner in hand, caught up in shared euphoria and momentary forgetfulness, dancers could stomp and swing themselves into states of [tranquility]. While the music's time surged forward, real-world time, paradoxically, seemed to stop. Ears flooded with irresistible melodies and intoxicating rhythms, skin flushed with excitement (and perhaps desire), and pulses quickened as [people danced] the nights, and their cares, away. . . . Most of the dancers were young people, and swing took center stage in American youth culture, just as rock and roll would two decades later. . . .

Bands had always competed for popularity, but in the Swing Era competition between dance bands came to the fore, taking on the characteristics of rivalry between great athletic teams. Bands attracted ardent followers, orchestras engaged in sometimes epic band battles, and jazz magazines and black newspapers ran readers' polls to select the top groups. Fans kept track of changes in bands' personnel and argued the merits of one band over another. . . .

[Swing] . . . affirmed the joys of dance, music, and youthful courtship; of risk-taking improvisation; of a dynamic African American force challenging and changing mainstream America. Like rock and roll would a generation later, swing drew young people powerfully, giving rise to a musical subculture. And swing affirmed the human spirit at a time when the country was still struggling to come out of the Great Depression.

such as Ella Fitzgerald, Sarah Vaughn, Billie Eckstine, Frank Sinatra, and Billie Holiday became more prominent as the swing era progressed into the 1940s. By the end of World War II, these vocalists were considered major attractions, and they took center stage while the bands simply acted as backup for their singing.

Dancing at the Savoy

Whether the attraction was the singer, the conductor, or the instrumentalists, there was little doubt that big-band swing had become a dominant form of popular entertainment. In *Jazz: The First Century,* John Edward Hasse describes how swing transformed American culture:

> Swing music and dancing became a huge phenomenon, almost a national obsession, taking jazz to heights of popularity never achieved before or since. More jazz musicians gained favor with the general public, more audiences turned to jazz as a backdrop for dancing and entertainment, than at any other time in history. Never before had jazz so dominated the field of popular music. At no other time was jazz such a catalyst for thousands of fans queuing up for a performance, for turn-away crowds so large and enthusiastic that the police had to be called in to keep order, for so many live radio broadcasts carrying the music to waiting listeners

coast-to-coast, and for heated band battles that became the stuff of legends. [30]

Big-band jazz was performed in glittering ballrooms known as dance palaces, which were decorated in the art deco style that featured geometric designs, bold colors, and artistic glass in chandeliers and mirrors. Inside the ballrooms, dance crazes rose and fell in popularity throughout the swing era. Dance steps with names such as the lindy hop, the Suzy Q, the shim-sham-shimmy, and the shag swept across the nation from the East Coast to the West.

Many of these steps originated with African American patrons of Harlem's Savoy Ballroom, whose nickname was "the Home of Happy Feet." [31]

Fletcher Henderson

Among those who played at the Savoy was pianist and composer Fletcher Henderson, who would play until 1:30 A.M. at the all-white Roseland Ballroom in New York City, then travel to Harlem to play at the Savoy until 3:30 in the morning. Henderson pioneered some of the fundamentals of big-band swing, such as contrasting reed and brass sections against one another and having band sections perform the call-and-response technique.

Musicians in Henderson's band were expected to read and play music expertly arranged by saxophonist Don Redman, Henderson's main arranger. At the same time, soloists interpreted songs in their own voice and impro-

Many dance steps like the lindy hop and the Suzy Q originated in Harlem's Savoy Ballroom, nicknamed "the Home of Happy Feet."

vised hot solos. Although Henderson's band was little known outside of New York, it served as a proving ground for many musicians who would go on to become stars in their own right, including trumpeter Cootie Williams, trombonists Charlie Green and Benny Morton, tenor saxophonist Chu Berry, and alto sax player Benny Carter.

Soon Henderson began offering some of his best arrangements, such as "King Porter Stomp," "Sometimes I'm Happy," and "Down South Camp Meeting" to Benny Goodman. Although these were huge hits, Henderson remained unknown to the general public. Despite Henderson's swing innovations,

his band struggled financially, finally breaking up in 1934.

Saxophone Solos

One of the most celebrated musicians to come out of Henderson's band was tenor sax player Coleman Hawkins. He had been hired by Henderson in 1923, when only eighteen years old, but remained with the bandleader for more than a decade.

When Hawkins first came along, the saxophone was rarely used in jazz. But the improvisational genius of Louis Armstrong on trumpet—and his ability to hit high notes—inspired Hawkins to make the saxophone a brilliant solo instrument, on par with the trumpet or clarinet. Giddens describes Hawkins's impact on jazz and the saxophone:

> Coleman Hawkins was the virtual inventor of the tenor saxophone in jazz. He was one of, to this day, one of the four or five greatest tenor saxophonists the music has ever produced. But he came along at a time when the tenor saxophone was a vaudeville clown's instrument, and no one had ever made serious music on it. [Maurice] Ravel and a few other [classical music] composers had attempted to write passages for the saxophone. . . . But Hawkins took the tenor saxophone and he made art on it. . . .
>
> He had the most virile sound I've ever heard on a tenor saxophone. It was big and full without being blustery, without a lot of wind or extra vibrato. And he just played with such authority, I mean every eight bars in a solo would just seem to . . . unfurl like a perfect ribbon. [There] . . . was never any hesitation or any question, any unnecessary repetition. Extraordinary eloquence.[32]

Hawkins found a rival in Lester Young, a New Orleans–based sax player who began his career playing in his family's traveling show. Young later joined the Blue Devils, a swing band that toured the Midwest, in what was

Coleman Hawkins proved that a musician could play serious music on the tenor saxophone.

known as a territory band because it confined its one-night stands to a certain geographic region.

Whereas Hawkins's style has been described as "hot," Young pioneered the "cool" jazz sound that was light, flowing, delicate, and used no vibrato.

Although his elegant style was panned by critics during the 1930s, Young's cool saxophone sound would be widely imitated by a later generation of musicians who played bebop-style jazz during the 1940s and 1950s.

Young gained national recognition after joining pianist Count Basie's band in 1934. And his 1936 recordings with Basie influenced countless other saxophone players, many of whom imitated Young's solos note for note.

Count Basie and the Kansas City Stomp

Young initially jammed with Basie in Kansas City, Missouri, where the growing jazz scene rivaled that in Chicago and New York. With a large African American population and a central location, Kansas City attracted hundreds of swing musicians from the East Coast, West Coast, North, and South. These musicians brought their own regional styles along with them. Playing a role similar to the one New Orleans had played in the early 1900s, Kansas City became a melting pot of jazz styles. Regardless of what style the musicians were used to playing, they were expected to perform any style, as competition was fierce. As jazz pianist Jay McShann said,

[If] you didn't swing in Kansas City, you hadn't said nothing. Then if you couldn't play . . . pretty, sweet music, like *Stardust* and stuff like that, you hadn't said anything. Then if you couldn't play boogie-woogie, you hadn't said anything. And if you couldn't play the blues, you hadn't said anything. See, in Kansas City you didn't just do one thing—you had to do the whole bit.[33]

Through the blending of this wide range of styles a new type of jazz emerged that combined boogie-woogie, blues, and swing. Known as stomp or jump blues, this eminently danceable music also featured "shout" vocals in which singers would boisterously yell out lyrics.

With his rapid-fire piano pounding, influenced by the stride playing of James P. Johnson, Basie was a leader among stomp jazz musicians. His compositions such as "One O'Clock Jump" and "Jumpin' at the Woodside" display a foot-stomping, finger-snapping beat that propels the horn solos forward with a rhythmic power that burns with an intensity unusual in swing jazz.

Basie's eight-piece band played a regular gig at the Reno Club in Kansas City throughout 1936, jamming nightly from 8:00 P.M. to 4:00 A.M. The shows were broadcast nationally over KXBY radio every night from 11:15 to 12:00 A.M., and this music caught the ear of New York producer John Hammond, who persuaded the talented composer to come to New York in early 1937, where he played an engagement at the Roseland Ballroom. Basie burst onto the national scene later that year when "One O'Clock Jump" became a hit on the national charts. In 1938 Basie's extended engagement at the Famous Door nightclub cemented his popularity and helped propel his composition "Stop Beatin' Round the Mulberry Bush" into the top ten.

Except for a brief period during the 1950s, Basie continuously led a big band from 1935 until his death fifty years later. He was one of the premier pianists, composers, and arrangers of the swing era, and his records were instant classics. And with their red-hot riffs jumping out of nearly every jukebox in the country, the players in Basie's orchestra were some of the most influential improvisers in the business.

The King of Swing

Basie's music was dynamic and imaginative, but the acknowledged king of swing during the mid-1930s was Benny Goodman. Although Goodman's music was not as adventurous and exciting as Basie's, his smooth, polished sound appealed to a larger audience.

Goodman has been given credit for kicking off the national swing craze in

The hit song "One O'Clock Jump" propelled Count Basie (seated at piano) to the top of the music charts in 1937.

John Hammond

John Hammond grew up in luxury in a huge New York City mansion with more than a dozen servants. But, as the following biography written by Scott Yanow and posted on the ARTISTdirect Network website confirms, Hammond's love of jazz made him one of swing's greatest promoters:

John Hammond Sr. was born on Dec. 15, 1910 in New York City. One of swing music's greatest [promoters], John Hammond was responsible for at least partly discovering a remarkable list of musicians through the years including Billie Holiday, Count Basie, Charlie Christian, George Benson, Aretha Franklin, Bob Dylan and Bruce Springsteen. Although these artists would certainly have made it on their own, Hammond's intervention made their rise to fame swifter. . . .

Although born into a wealthy family and educated at Yale, John Hammond from nearly the start had a great love for black music. As early as 1933 (when he was 22), Hammond was active in the music business, discovering Billie Holiday and getting her into the recording studio, producing Bessie Smith's final sessions and becoming a friend of the young Benny Goodman (who would marry Hammond's sister).

Hammond produced freewheeling American jazz sessions for the European market, worked with Fletcher Henderson . . . and encouraged Goodman to form his first big band. In 1935 he teamed Lady Day [Billie Holiday] with pianist Teddy Wilson for a series of classic recordings, the next year he discovered Count Basie's orchestra while randomly scanning the radio dial (he soon flew to Kansas City and encouraged Basie to come East). . . .

After hearing about [groundbreaking jazz guitarist] Charlie Christian in 1939, Hammond took a plane to Oklahoma City, listened to the young guitarist for himself and flew him to Los Angeles where he had Christian audition for an initially reluctant Benny Goodman.

1934 when he put together his first twelve-piece band using Henderson as his arranger. Goodman wanted to perfect a sound that would reach out to young people, who he recognized were a key audience who filled dance halls and who purchased a majority of records. To attract this group, Goodman believed a swing band still needed to have a small-combo sound. He later recalled, "I was

With a sound that appealed to a mass audience, Benny Goodman became widely regarded as the king of swing in the 1930s.

interested only in jazz. I wanted to create a tight, small-band quality, and I wanted every one of my boys to be a soloist. The band had to have a driving beat, a rhythmic brass section, and a sax section that would be smooth with lots of punch."[34] Goodman achieved the sound he was hoping for, hiring players such as Bunny Berigan on trumpet, Jess Stacey on piano, Helen Ward on vocals, and revolutionary beat wizard Gene Krupa on drums.

Goodman's band was hired to perform at Billy Rose's Music Hall in New York, playing the last hour of a three-hour show that was broadcast nationally over NBC radio. This show helped Goodman sell many records, and he had nearly a dozen top-ten hits, including "Moonglow" and "Bugle Call Rag."

Goodman's popularity really took off when, using his growing reputation as a springboard, Goodman and his band set off on a cross-country tour in 1935. The response was at first disappointing; Goodman's brand of smooth, cool swing did not appeal to Great Depression-era listeners in small towns, who wanted to hear ballads, waltzes, and other traditional music. Goodman was even ready to break up the band, but then they reached the Palomar Ballroom in Los Angeles on August 21, 1935.

When Goodman broke into his trademark sound, the students in the sold-out audience went wild, nearly causing a riot. After this engagement, Goodman traveled to Chicago, then to New York, where, once again, near riots accompanied his playing. From that point on, Goodman was gold. He scored dozens of top-ten hits and played the prestigious Carnegie Hall at a time when swing had never been heard in a concert-hall setting. Goodman's band quickly spawned popular offshoots. Band members such as super showman Gene Krupa and trumpeter Harry James became so famous that they started their own bands to capitalize on the swing craze.

One of the lasting effects of Goodman's popularity was the breaking down of racial barriers. The Jewish clarinetist openly admired African American jazz musicians. Using his popularity as a cushion from racist critics, Goodman put together one of the first racially mixed bands in 1935, beginning with African American Teddy Wilson on piano, and later adding Lionel Hampton on vibes, and string virtuoso Charlie Christian on electric guitar. While other black bands sometimes had white musicians sit in, Goodman's was the first white-led band to employ African American artists in concert settings.

Ella Fitzgerald Sings and Swings

Goodman's band broke with tradition in another way as well. When he hired singer Helen Ward, there were few swing bands with female vocalists. But Goodman correctly assumed that Ward's presence would help his band reach out to a younger crowd—and attract male college students to his gigs.

With the stunning success of Goodman's band, other bands eagerly hired female singers. Down at the Savoy Ballroom, drummer Chick Webb hired Ella Fitzgerald in 1935. Fitzgerald was an unlikely candidate for jazz stardom.

Legendary jazz singer Ella Fitzgerald performs at the Savoy Ballroom.

She had been living in poverty on the streets of New York when, on a dare, she entered an amateur talent contest at Harlem's Apollo Theater in 1934. After winning the twenty-five dollar prize money for her clean, clear vocal style, she was introduced to Webb, who reluctantly agreed to hire the inexperienced singer for one night. The crowd loved Fitzgerald's beautiful voice, and Webb kept her on for a week-long engagement at the Savoy. Before long, Fitzgerald was recording with the Chick Webb Orchestra, and over half the band's selections featured the vocalist.

In 1938 Fitzgerald converted the nursery rhyme "A-tisket, A-tasket" into a huge hit record for Webb. This was soon followed by "Undecided." By this time, the singer was developing the unmatched improvisation and scat abilities that would define her long, illustrious career.

Billie Holiday Is Lady Day

Although Fitzgerald had a long, brilliant career singing with nearly every swing star from Louis Armstrong to Count Basie, her career was eclipsed during the swing era by Lady Day—Billie Holiday.

Holiday forever changed jazz vocalizing as surely as Armstrong had transformed trumpet playing. In fact, Lady Day adapted Satchmo's vocal phrasings and rhythms, as Hasse writes:

Billie Holiday ranks close to Louis Armstrong among the greatest jazz singers. Acknowledging great inspiration from him, she practiced an instrumental approach to singing as she ranged freely over the beat, flattened out the melodic contours of tunes, and, in effect, recomposed songs to suit her range, style, and artistic sensibilities. Her voice was physically limited [in range], but she achieved shadings, nuances, color, and variety by sliding along the thin line separating speech and song. Her collaborations with Lester Young (*I Must Have That Man* and *This Year's Kisses,* both recorded with Teddy Wilson's group, 1937) are justifiably celebrated, as is her courageous recording of the harrowing anti-lynching song *Strange Fruit* (1939) and her haunting studio recording, with strings, of *Lover Man* (1944).[35]

Audiences were attracted to Holiday's almost girlish voice, which belied a melancholy blues and sweet vulnerability deep in her soul. She personalized songs as if they were written specifically for her, and she wrote some classics herself, including "God Bless the Child."

Lady Day's life and career, filled with sexual abuse and drug addiction, was like something out of a low-down blues song. She had been abused as a child and turned to prostitution at a young age. As a singer, she was terrified of the stage, but she used her talents to

Jazz Goes to War

In Jazz: A History of America's Music, *Geoffrey C. Ward describes the effect World War II had on swing music:*

On December 7, 1941, America found itself at war. Jazz went to war, too, and overseas, swing—still America's most popular music—would serve to remind the men and women of the armed forces of home. "Bandsmen today are not just jazz musicians," said [jazz magazine] *Down Beat,* "they are soldiers of music."

On the home front, the music industry found itself struggling again. Blackouts and late-night curfews darkened some nightclubs and dance halls. A 20 percent entertainment tax closed ballrooms all across the country. The rationing of rubber and gasoline eventually drove most band buses off the roads, and servicemen now filled the Pullman trains, making it difficult for musicians to get around by rail. . . . [Companies] stopped making jukeboxes and musical instruments altogether for a time because they were deemed unnecessary to the war effort.

The draft stole away good musicians—Jack Teagarden lost 17 men to the army in just four months. He and other bandleaders were forced to pay their replacements more for less talent. "I'm paying some kid trumpet player $500 a week," Tommy Dorsey complained, "and he can't even blow his nose." . . .

By October 1942, *Down Beat* was running a regular column headed Killed in Action. At one point during the fighting, there were 39 bandleaders enlisted in the Army, 17 in the Navy, three in the Merchant Marine, and two more in the Coast Guard. Glenn Miller, whose infectious swing hits like *In the Mood* epitomized the war years, disbanded his own hugely successful orchestra to form an all-star Air Force unit—and perished when his airplane disappeared over the English Channel. . . .

Artie Shaw led a Navy band that toured the South Pacific—playing in jungles so hot and humid that the pads on the saxophones rotted and horns had to be held together with rubber bands.

escape the streets. She made it big, singing with Goodman in 1933, Basie in 1937, and clarinetist Artie Shaw in 1938. After deciding to pursue a solo career in 1939, Holiday enjoyed great popularity. However, drug and alcohol addiction destroyed her health, and she died in 1959 at the age of forty-four.

The End of the Big Bands

Despite the popularity of performers like Billie Holiday, big-band jazz was hit hard when, in 1941, the United States entered World War II. Shortages of basic goods such as shellac, which was used at that time to make records, put an end to the recording business for a few years. Shortages of gasoline and tires due to rationing took the touring bands off the road. Even brass and silver, used to make musical instruments, were in short supply. Musicians, too, were scarce, as hundreds of men were drafted or volunteered for military service.

The swing bands that remained intact joined in the war effort, playing concerts for U.S. troops throughout North America and Europe. Some jazz entertainers gave more than their time and talents. One of the greatest band leaders, Glenn Miller, died on his way to a show when his plane went down over the English Channel on December 14, 1944.

The end of the war in 1945 brought no recovery for the big-band business. The wild teenagers who lindy hopped their blues away during the Great Depression had grown up, and as millions of soldiers returned home, dancing and swinging gave way to buying homes, raising babies, and going to work. In December 1946, eight top bandleaders—Woody Herman, Benny Goodman, Harry James, Les Brown, Jack Teagarden, Benny Carter, Ina Ray Hutton, and Tommy Dorsey—announced they were quitting the business. The sounds of big-band swing that had once rung through the streets and alleys of cities large and small faded to silence.

Chapter Four

The Birth of Bebop

A t the beginning of the 1940s, the big-band swing music of Benny Goodman, Woody Herman, and Glenn Miller was blasting out of radios, jukeboxes, and ballrooms across the nation. But the public's taste was volatile, and within a few years jazz music entered a period of rapid change.

After the end of World War II, big-band swing was deemed passé by the record-buying public; the sounds that had been popular during the Great Depression years seemed irrelevant to many in the prosperous postwar period. As the majority of Americans married, settled down, and had children, they began to listen to romantic ballads that featured smooth-voiced crooners like Frank Sinatra, who sang catchy melodies backed by lush string orchestras. Even innovative jazz singers such as Ella Fitzgerald and Sarah Vaughn began to record mainstream pop music so that they could survive in the rapidly changing music business.

And even more changes were in store by the mid-1950s, when a new style of music, rock and roll, shook the music business—and popular culture—to its very foundations. With performers such as Elvis Presley, Chuck Berry, and Little Richard dominating the airwaves, the music of the elegant Ellington and the innovative Armstrong seemed to belong to ancient history.

New Sounds, New Scales

As the commercial demand for big-band music evaporated, black jazz instrumentalists began to gather in smoky barrooms in New York City to jam. Liberated from the constraints of trying to please mainstream audiences, musicians at these sessions broke the traditional rules of swing, introducing new concepts to create a style of jazz that came to be known as bop or bebop.

The term for the style is taken from a tune by trumpeter Dizzy Gillespie, "Bebop," recorded in 1945. The sound differed from big-band swing in many significant ways: Bebop was played by small combos, as opposed to large bands. The tempo of bebop was fast—in its most frenzied form, it was almost twice as fast as the average swing dance tune. Bebop featured trumpets, saxophones, standup basses, drums, and pianos but rarely the clarinet, which had been so prominent in swing music. And the drums, instead of providing a steady background beat, constantly interacted with the horns.

Bebop musicians valued innovation, improvisation, and hot licks above all else. And to play bebop, a musician had to be extremely proficient on his instrument—more so than had been the case with swing—since the melodies, harmonies, and rhythms of the music were much more complex. In addition, the music was based solely on improvisation, there were few written musical arrangements, and if there was a score, it was used more as a rough outline rather than as a detailed blueprint for the musicians.

At the most basic level, bebop was different since it used a different musical scale from the one traditionally employed in Western music. Whereas earlier jazz melodies and harmonies had been based on the seven-note (diatonic) scale, bebop was chromatic—that is, it utilized all twelve notes of the scale. Some listeners considered the music discordant, but this change greatly increased the range of the jazz soloist.

Although bebop was a delight to sophisticated listeners, it was most definitely not dance music. In fact, its speedy tempos and shifting beats frightened away many dancers. And while sax and trumpet players might have been excited by the cascading and surprising licks, it was not music the average listener found relaxing to hear.

Jamming at Minton's

Just as earlier advances in jazz may be traced to a few innovative players such as Armstrong and Ellington, the birth of bebop and modern jazz may be attributed to Gillespie, saxophonist Charlie Parker, pianist Thelonious Monk, and drummer Kenny Clarke. These men, in turn, had been influenced by swing players such as saxophonists Lester Young and Coleman Hawkins, pianist Art Tatum, guitarist Charlie Christian, and bassist Jimmy Blanton.

The pioneers of bebop began their careers in swing bands led by Cab Calloway, Earl Hines, and Billy Eckstine. After an evening of performing in front of white crowds, the jazz innovators often traveled to Harlem nightclubs after hours to jam. Since most players did not have the freedom to let their creative juices flow during their regular performances, Harlem jams often turned into cutting sessions where experimentation was the rule.

Monday nights, when few jazz musicians had any gigs at all, turned out to be particularly productive when it came to innovation. During the late 1940s, in order to attract a crowd on the slowest night of the week, the manager of a Harlem club called Minton's offered free food and drink to musicians who would come in and play. Before long, these open stage jams began to attract the hippest crowds in New York.

The house band at Minton's consisted of Clarke, Monk, bassist Nick Fenton, and trumpet player Joe Guy. They were often joined by Gillespie and Parker. As word of these jam sessions spread, New York's finest players would make the pilgrimage to Harlem on Monday nights. But the competition at Minton's was brutal. Musicians who were not of the first rank were often blown off the stage by the house band's players, who would change keys, play at difficult rhythms, or use other tricks to separate the truly talented from the hopeful amateurs. Out-of-towners also were grist for the mill as pianist Hampton Hawes recalls:

One night at Minton's . . . somebody recognized me and said, "There's a cat from California supposed to play good, let's get him up here." Now at that time there were a lot of East Coast musicians who thought it slick to try to shoot down anyone new on the scene who was starting to make a reputation. It was like an initiation, a ceremonial rite . . . calling far-out tunes in strange keys with the hip changes at tempos so fast if you didn't fly you fell—that's

Trumpeter Dizzy Gillespie (second from left) was among the early pioneers of modern jazz. The musical style known as bebop was named after one of his tunes.

Jazz on the Street

New York's Fifty-second Street was lined with so many jazz clubs that it was known simply as "the Street" by musicians and fans alike. This center of jazz is described by Tad Lathrop in Jazz: The First Century, *edited by John Edward Hasse:*

It was called "Swing Street" and "the street that never slept." In its nightclub heyday—which lasted roughly from 1933 to the late forties—the stretch of Manhattan's 52nd Street that ran between Fifth and Seventh Avenues served as a vibrant center of jazz activity.

Clubs such as the Onyx, the Famous Door, and the Three Deuces lit the street in neon. Over time, they also cast light on the changing face of jazz. In the late thirties, a walk past a club marquee and downstairs into a basement would plunge a visitor into a crowded, smoke-filled setting alive with the sounds of swing. Ten years later, that same descent would emerge the clubgoer in the hyperkinetic energy of bebop.

The Street offered a grab bag of options for fans and players alike. On any given night, a jazz seeker could snake from one brownstone to another and catch sets by Art Tatum, Coleman Hawkins, and Billie Holiday. The musicians themselves would hop from club to club, finishing up their regular shows and then rushing across the street or a couple of doors away to sit in with other bands. With new ideas and players circulating freely, tested for durability in late-night "cutting sessions," 52nd Street became a hothouse of innovation and involving styles.

It was on the Street that many heard sax innovator Charlie Parker for the first time, when he would drop in unannounced to jam. . . . Parker's influence would course through the Street's echoing basements and into future jazz.

how you earned your diploma in the University of the Streets of New York.

For a week I had watched these cats burning each other up, ambushing outsiders, [messing] up their minds so bad they would fold and split the stand after one tune. Surprised by their coldness because they were so friendly off the stand, I [guessed] that I wasn't quite ready. . . . No point in selling tickets if you don't have a show. [36]

"Klook-Mop" Clarke Rides a New Rhythm

One innovation was the direct result of this effort to weed out all but the best musicians. Kenny Clarke was the leader of Minton's house band, and the drummer spurred on the soloists—and made their lives difficult—with unusual hits and accents that broke up the tempo while kicking the music into high gear. Until this time, jazz drummers generally kept up a steady beat using their foot pedal on the big bass drum. Clarke shifted the rhythm to a quick tapping of his ride cymbal. In *The Birth of Bebop* by Scott DeVeaux, Clarke describes how he inadvertently developed this technique:

> It just happened sort of accidentally. . . . We were playing a real fast tune once with Teddy Hill—"Old Man River," I think—and the tempo was too fast to play four beats to the measure, so I began to cut the time up. But to keep the same rhythm going, I had to do it with my hand [on the cymbal], because my foot just wouldn't do it [on the bass drum]. So I started doing it with my hand, and then every once in a while I would kind of lift myself with my foot, to kind of boot myself into it. . . .
>
> When it was over, I said, "Good God, was that ever hard." So then I began to think, and say, "Well, you know, it worked. It worked and nobody said anything, so it came out right. So that must be

the way to do it." Because I think if I had been able to do it [the old way], it would have been stiff. It wouldn't have worked. [37]

Clarke's revved-up cymbal riding soon earned him the nickname "Klook-Mop," or "Klook," a word that loosely sounded like Clarke's drumbeat: *bop-klook-mop, klook-mop.*

Kenny Clarke created a new drumming style by using a ride cymbal rather than a foot pedal to keep a steady beat.

Groovin' High with Gillespie

As fate would have it, Clarke's new groove dovetailed perfectly with the inventive trumpet playing of Dizzy Gillespie, who had come to New York to play with Cab Calloway's band during the late 1930s.

Gillespie almost single-handedly invented bebop by introducing a note called a flatted fifth to the standard diatonic scale. What this meant was that in whatever scale was used as the basis for a composition, the fifth note in the scale would be played as a flat. For example, a normal C scale would be C-D-E-F-G-A-B; in this scale the G would be played as a G-flat. Using a flatted-fifth scale provides a dark, moody sound, which was called devil's music during the eighteenth century. But according to Gillespie, "With the flatted fifth I really got turned on. . . . I was excited about the progression and used it everywhere."[38]

Using this scale as a basis for his jams, Gillespie rearranged the language of jazz and became one of the most respected players of the modern era. His astounding chops were matched by his talents for composition. Gillespie wrote dozens of pieces, including "Salt Peanuts," "Groovin' High," "Blue 'n' Boogie," and "A Night in Tunisia," which became instant bebop standards. As Gridley writes,

> Dizzy Gillespie's harmonic skills were startling, and he flaunted them. His phrases were full of surprises and playful changes of direction. He could precariously go in and out of keys within a single phrase, always managing to resolve the unexpected at the next chord. He often zoomed up to the trumpet's high register during the middle of a phrase and still managed to connect the melodic ideas logically. . . . And despite its complexity, his work bristled with excitement. . . .
>
> Gillespie would occasionally toy with a single note, playing it again and again, each time in a different way, creating different rhythmic patterns and using changes in loudness and tone color to achieve variety in his sound. One Gillespie method . . . is to make the trumpet tone brittle and then crack it resoundingly in a burst of high notes. Also . . . he could channel all his terrific energy into a ballad, using his exceptional skill with harmony, his fertile imagination, and virtuoso technique to mold a unique, personal creation.[39]

Gillespie was also responsible for introducing the Afro-Cuban sound to jazz by hiring Caribbean-born conga player Chano Pozo in 1947. Pozo did not speak a word of English, and Gillespie did not speak Spanish, but Gillespie was fascinated by the complex rhythmic patterns, known as polyrhythms, that were prominent in Cuban music. In his autobiography *To Be or Not to Bop,* Gillespie describes how Pozo taught his band the rhythms on the tour bus:

On the bus, he'd give me a drum, [bass player] Al McKibbon a drum, and he'd take a drum. Another guy would have a cowbell, and he'd give everybody a rhythm [to play]. We'd see how all the rhythms tied into one another, and everybody was playing something different. We'd be on the road in a bus, riding down the road, and we'd sing and play all down the highway. He'd teach us some of those Cuban chants and things like that. That's how I learned to play the congas. [40]

Gillespie was the first jazz bandleader to utilize these exciting rhythms on songs such as "Cubano Bop" and "Manteca." He called this new style of jazz Cubop because it combined Cuban rhythms and bebop, a marriage of Caribbean dance music and American jazz. Gillespie promoted Cubop relentlessly to show that bebop could also be dance music, but the general public remained unconvinced. Although his music was not appreciated by a large audience, Gillespie's appearance became synonymous with bebop. His cheeks puffed out like balloons when he blew his horn, whose bell was bent up so that it would achieve a louder tone. He was always seen in stylish suits and wore a goatee; black, thick-rimmed "bop" glasses; and black berets. Gillespie used beatnik slang, spoke like a "hepcat," and the press loved him.

Instead of accepting the fact that the general public was alienated by his

Gillespie was the first bandleader to integrate Afro-Cuban sounds into jazz.

hard-to-comprehend music, Gillespie promoted the music as something anyone could enjoy. During the late 1950s he took bebop on a worldwide promotional tour, playing extensively in Japan, Europe, South America, and elsewhere. During the sixties Gillespie continued to bop with small combos.

In all, Gillespie has been credited with changing jazz in three important aspects: He created a unique trumpet style that showcased his virtuosity and redefined the possibilities of the instrument; as an ambassador of bebop to the world, he legitimized it as a real musical style; and Gillespie changed the dynamics between jazz musicians. Whereas many players had been afraid to reveal their secrets, even playing with their backs to the others, Gillespie shared, taught, and encouraged others to reach the pinnacle of their talents.

The Bird Sings

Gillespie, the expressive emissary of bop, found his foil in saxophonist Charlie "Bird" Parker, an introverted mystery of a man. Parker was born in 1920 and grew up playing in that crossroads of music, Kansas City. Raised on blues, ragtime, and jump, Parker pursued music recklessly and relentlessly, jamming all night every night. Fueled by the amphetamine called Benzedrine, Bird blew his sax in a high-speed cascade of notes, perfecting a style called doubling up, in which melodies were played at twice the written tempo.

By the mid-1940s Parker was a regular fixture at Minton's and the jazz clubs on New York's Fifty-second Street. He had been jamming with Gillespie since 1942, and their 1945 duet of the song "Salt Peanuts" laid out the future of bebop in its breakneck melodies. Music critic Gary Giddens describes Parker's genius:

Charlie Parker was like a prophet when he first came on the scene, right at the end of the Second World War. . . . [His music] was explosive, out of nowhere. . . . It was shocking, the way Louis Armstrong was shocking in the 1920s. I mean . . . where did this come from, this speed, the velocity, the excitement, the exhilaration? . . . [It's] melody, but it's played so fast, and with such joy and such exhilaration that it totally revolutionized the music. . . .

He broke through the basic chord system that was common in jazz, started playing on the upper intervals, and brought a whole new spontaneity and melodic vocabulary to music. . . . It's a magical thing and it's only happened relatively few times in the history of western civilization where a musician comes along and can completely transmute the music. [41]

Between 1945 and 1955 Parker was the king of bebop saxophone, with a legion of admirers within the jazz community. Unfortunately, he received little critical acclaim in the mainstream media. Whereas Gillespie danced, sang, and appealed to a large audience, Parker haunted the dingy clubs of New York, strung out on heroin, toting his alto saxophone in a paper bag tied up with rubber bands. He was sometimes mistaken for a hobo until he took out his battered horn and began to play. Then, with almost superhuman concentration, Bird let fly with a burst of notes while appearing to sit stock-still behind his sunglasses.

Unfortunately, many musicians who were Parker's fans thought that they could play like Bird if they too took heroin. By the midfifties dozens of jazz's greatest players had descended into the hell of addiction. Parker himself struggled mightily before dying in 1955 at the age of thirty-four. And the drugs and alcohol had taken their toll: The doctor who examined Bird's lifeless body thought he was looking at a man in his sixties.

Charlie "Bird" Parker's extraordinary musical career was cut short by his death at the age of thirty-four.

Thelonious Monk— Melodious Thunk

Along with Parker and Gillespie, another important piece of the bebop puzzle was the pianist with the unlikely name of Thelonious Sphere Monk, born in 1917. (He often joked that with the middle name of "Sphere" no one would ever call him a square.) Monk, born in North Carolina and raised in New York City, was a regular in the jazz scene, joining Clarke's house band at Minton's around 1940.

Like Gillespie, Monk was a composer whose characteristic tunes, such as "Straight No Chaser" and "Round Midnight," became bebop standards. And while playing bebop on the piano, Monk specialized in accenting melodies in odd places and ending musical phrases with unexpected notes in a surprising flourish. In technical terms described by writer Kenny Mathieson, Monk played "highly original harmonic progressions, dissonant intervals and oblique, angular rhythms."[42] Monk was famed for his use of flatted third chords, also called half-diminished chords, which leaves the music sounding unresolved. Monk's compositions were intellectually complex, but he also wove humor into his music. For example, in the middle of the bebop number "Sweet and Lovely," Monk plays the traditional ditty "Tea for Two."

As an enigmatic master behind the keys, Monk was misunderstood, even within the bebop community. He liked unusual hats, and he would often make

Parker's Dangerous Appetites

Charlie "Bird" Parker began shooting heroin by the age of seventeen, and his appetite for drugs was legendary. While playing in swing bands, Bird perfected the technique of dozing behind his sunglasses, with his cheeks puffed out so it would look like he was playing, even though he was really in a heroin-induced stupor. When it came time for his solo, he instructed a band mate to jab him in the leg with a pin to wake him up. The Public Broadcasting System's online article "American Masters— Charlie Parker," provides details of Bird's tragic career:

D ue in part to dissatisfaction with [a lack of critical acclaim] and in part to his years of on and off drug use, Parker slipped into serious addiction. On a two-year tour of California, his drinking and drug addiction worsened, and for six months he was in a Los Angeles rehabilitation center.

It was not until his tour of Europe that Parker began to receive the at-tention he deserved. . . . However, as continuing personal and creative pressures mounted, he went into a tailspin: drinking, behaving errati-cally, and even being banned from "Birdland," the legendary 52nd Street club named in his honor. Throughout this time, however, one thing remained intact—Parker's playing continued to exhibit the same technical genius and emo-tional investment that had made him great.

In 1954, while working again in California, Parker learned of the death of his two-year-old daughter, and went into further decline . . . re-duced to playing in dives. The cheap red wine he had become addicted to was exacerbating his stomach ulcers, and he even once attempted suicide. On March 9, 1955, while visiting his friend . . . Charlie Parker died. The coroner cited pneumonia as the cause, and estimated Parker's age at fifty-five or sixty. He was only thirty-four.

odd little dances around his grand pi-ano. These steps looked foolish to some, but in the process Monk was ac-tually conducting the band, showing them the rhythm.

Monk demonstrated that great mu-sic is not just the notes played but the notes *not played* as well. He often left silent spaces in his compositions, causing some who were used to the rapid-fire riffs of Gillespie and Parker to assume Monk could not play very well. But as jazz pianist De Wild ex-plains,

[Monk] taught the science of the maximum economy in the choice of the notes making up a chord. Why play three when two were enough! And that's another torture for whomever tries to reproduce Monk's music: you always think you're hearing more notes than he's actually playing. [43]

Monk was never easy to understand. Many times he was totally introverted and refused to communicate with any-

one. When he did speak, his convoluted and eccentric pronouncements were understood by few. During the late 1940s and 1950s Monk struggled professionally, but he was suddenly elevated to celebrity status in 1957 by a crowd of young nonconformists called beatniks who appreciated his unique brand of music.

Monk toured extensively throughout the sixties and early seventies, but he retired suddenly in 1973, suffering from mental illness. He spent the rest

Though he struggled in obscurity for many years, pianist Thelonious Monk became a celebrity when a crowd of nonconformists known as the beatniks discovered his unique style.

of his life in seclusion but proved one remarkable fact about his music: It was born fully formed, and from the time he began playing in the late forties until his retirement more than twenty-five years later, he saw no need to alter his style. As the great pianist himself simply said, "I wanted to play my own chords. I wanted to create and invent."[44]

The Birth of Modern Jazz

By the early fifties, bebop was the predominant style of jazz, blasting out of clubs from coast to coast. In addition to the sounds of Klook-Mop, Dizzy, Bird, and Monk, the music could be heard in the recordings of sax players Dexter Gordon, Stan Getz, and Sonny Rollins, in the drumming of Max Roach, in the

Bop and the Beat Generation

The 1950s spawned a movement of mostly white nonconformists who called themselves beatniks or the beat generation. Beat authors included Jack Kerouac, Allen Ginsberg, William Burroughs, and others. In the following article, "Jazz and the Beat Generation," Mike Janssen describes why the beboppers and beats were kindred spirits:

Jack Kerouac, Allen Ginsberg and friends spent much of their time in New York clubs . . . shooting the breeze and digging the music. Charlie Parker, Dizzy Gillespie and Miles Davis rapidly became what Allen Ginsberg dubbed "Secret Heroes" to this group of [music lovers]. . . .

The Beat authors borrowed many . . . terms from the jazz/hipster slang of the '40s, peppering their works with words such as "square," "cats," "nowhere," and "dig." But jazz meant much more than just a vocab-

ulary to the Beat writers. To them, jazz was a way of life, a completely different way to approach the creative process. . . .

Not only did the Beats . . . try to emulate the ways of life of bebop greats, they used the principal ideas of bebop playing and applied it to prose and poetry writing, creating a style sometimes called "bop prosody." Beat prose, especially that of Jack Kerouac, is characterized by a style submerged in the stream of consciousness, words blurted out in vigorous bursts, rarely revised and often sparsely punctuated for lines and lines. "No periods . . . but the vigorous space dash separating rhetorical breathing (as jazz musician drawing breath between outblown phrases)" wrote Jack Kerouac in his "Essentials of Spontaneous Prose," one of the few pieces he wrote which explained his method of writing.

Bebop musicians like saxophonist Dexter Gordon had a wild, freewheeling sound that was foreign to most mainstream Americans in the 1950s.

piano stylings of Bud Powell and Billy Taylor, in the guitar playing of Barney Kessel, in the arrangements of Gil Evans, and so many others.

Although they never were highly successful in the commercial sense of large record sales, these jazz musicians blew a cool, wild, and free sound whose spirit was seriously lacking in other aspects of American life during the 1950s. Perhaps this is the reason that bebop was adopted by various hepcats, beatniks, and nonconformists in general. Bop was music played by people who faced discrimination and prejudice in almost every aspect of their daily lives. With fast-paced changes, complex rhythms and melodies, and improvised virtuosity, bop profoundly influenced American culture and spawned several styles, such as free jazz, cool jazz, and hard bop, that remain an important part of jazz history.

Chapter Five

The Cool, the Hard, and the Free

M odern jazz developed from the bebop movement of the late 1940s and early 1950s, and by the late fifties the music had blasted off in three distinct directions: cool jazz, hard bop, and free jazz.

The mellow, laid-back sounds of cool jazz were to a great extent a reaction to the fast-paced, often dissonant music of bebop. Listeners found cool jazz—influenced by swing and even classical music—melodious and inviting. It is sometimes called the West Coast style when identified with white musicians who played it in California. Above all, cool jazz was played by musicians who were "cool" in the sense of being in control, poised, unhurried, and unruffled.

The Birth of Cool Jazz

At the end of the 1940s, while Dizzy Gillespie and Charlie "Bird" Parker were revolutionizing jazz with the sounds of bebop, pianist Claude Thornhill was touring the country with a

dance band that employed instruments more commonly found in a symphony orchestra, such as French horns, bassoons, and even tubas. Gil Evans, the band's arranger, seized on the idea of utilizing the unique tone colors of these instruments in a modern jazz setting. In 1948 Evans shared his idea of a lighter, more orchestral sounding jazz with a young trumpet player, Miles Davis. Together they created a seminal new sound.

Davis, who was born in 1926 and grew up in East St. Louis, Illinois, had honed his chops playing with Parker during the mid-1940s. By the late forties Davis was pursuing a solo career, and between 1949 and 1950 Davis recorded a series of cool jazz songs that would later be put together on the album *The Birth of the Cool.*

Davis recorded the album using a nine-piece band of bebop musicians that included drummer Kenny Clarke, trombonist J.J. Johnson, alto saxophonist Lee Konitz, baritone saxophonist Gerry Mulligan, pianist John Lewis, bassist Al McKibbon, and others. The cool jazz sound was a result of Evans's songlike arrangements that meshed perfectly with Davis's sweet trumpet tone and lyrical improvisations.

The record featured smooth bebop riffs over relaxed, subdued background arrangements that gave it a large orchestral sound with a minimum number of instruments. Critic Gary Giddens describes the background music as "big, cloud-like harmonies where all the instruments would come together in these huge chords that just seemed to float in the air."[45] Meanwhile, the solos were shorter, the music was highly organized, and the ensemble sound was emphasized. The sound was not loud or brassy as in bebop. Davis later described his playing style during this period:

Miles Davis ushered in the era of cool jazz, a style that used relaxed background arrangements and a minimum number of instruments.

The "Cool School" of Miles Davis

Miles Davis is one of the most enigmatic figures in jazz, almost as well known for his temperamental personality as for his distinctive and original music. In Jazz: The First Century, *edited by John Edward Hasse, Neil Tesser discusses the music of this pioneer of cool jazz, hard bop, and free jazz:*

Miles Davis, more than any other single musician, dominated the [modern jazz] era. . . . It was during [the 1950s] that he first evidenced the ability to synthesize emerging jazz sounds into coherent styles that others would embrace as new movements—an ability that would ultimately make Davis the most important jazz figure in the second half of the twentieth century, in the minds of many. . . .

Davis played introspective solos in a vulnerable, [hesitant] trumpet voice, which boasted virtually none of bebop's trademark fireworks and clever one-upsmanship. Old-school trumpeters derided his technique, but Davis's style became the template for jazz expression among musicians and audiences for the next twenty years. . . .

Davis often turned his back on his audience or left the bandstand entirely when not soloing. . . . And he turned his back on jazz entirely as the 1950s began, dropping out of sight and sound for the better part of two years to overcome the heroin habit he'd learned from [Charlie] Parker. But even in absentia, Davis wielded influence: the "cool school" inspired by his. . . . recordings became the "new sound of jazz." By the time Davis returned to the scene in 1953, "cool" had begun seeping up from the jazz underground to become the primary concern of American art, from film to fashion to literature to theater. From 1954 on, Davis's bands would brilliantly capture the hard-bop style, but his own trumpet work never abandoned the hooded stance that characterized cool jazz.

I think what they really meant [by cool] was a soft sound. . . . Not penetrating too much. To play soft you have to relax. . . . You don't delay the beat, but you might play a [group of notes] that *sounds* delayed. . . . I always wanted to play with a light sound, because I could think better when I played that way. [46]

Although *The Birth of the Cool* was not released by Capitol Records in album form until 1957, the twelve tracks on it were released as individual records. Although they did not sell very well at first, the musicians who appeared on the records went on to pursue the cool jazz sound, influencing many in California. Meanwhile, Davis abandoned cool jazz almost as soon as he pioneered it, ever searching for a new and different sound.

Cool Moves West

The cool sound moved west when, after working in New York with Davis and Evans, Gerry Mulligan moved to Los Angeles, where he put together a quartet with Chet Baker, whose trumpet tone often resembled the moody, cool sound of Miles Davis. With a bass player and drummer, Mulligan took the cool sound and gave it a new flavor by adding elements of New Orleans jazz, swing, and bop. As Geoffrey C. Ward writes in *Jazz: A History of America's Music,* "The quartet's sound was rollicking, breezy, and good-humored, inviting to those who found bebop forbidding." [47]

After working with Miles Davis and Gil Evans in New York, Gerry Mulligan brought the sound of cool jazz to the West Coast.

The move west gave cool jazz the break it needed. As fate would have it, a reporter from *Time* heard the quartet at a Los Angeles club called the Haig and wrote a glowing article for the magazine. *Time* called the music unique and even compared it to the music of baroque composer Johann Sebastian Bach. The positive review prompted Los Angeles radio stations to play the quartet's cool jazz recordings of songs such as "Walkin' Shoes" and

"Line for Lyons" on the radio. Although not as danceable as swing, the music was something to which people could shake their heads and tap their feet. Before long, Mulligan and Baker were national jazz stars.

Meanwhile, other California musicians, particularly sax player Jimmy Giuffre, flutist and alto sax player Bud Shank, and trumpeter Shorty Roger, began to experiment with the new sound, which the press dubbed the West Coast cool school. Drummer Shelly Manne described the goals of the cool school musicians:

> What we wanted to do . . . was write some new kind of material for jazz musicians, where the solos and the improvisations became part of the whole, and you couldn't tell where the writing ended and the improvisations began. . . . [It] was lighter, maybe a little more "laid-back." [48]

West Coast was not for everybody, however. Almost all of the major jazz magazines, including *Down Beat,* were based in New York. And the East Coast critics considered West Coast cool lightweight and unimaginative, more of a movie soundtrack for the sunny California lifestyle than a serious art form. However, the record-buying public—which cared little about such matters—loved it because of its easygoing tone and accessible melodies. In fact, *Down Beat* readers voted Baker the best trumpet player in the country in 1955.

Brubeck Takes Five

Whereas the Mulligan and Baker quartet popularized the cool sound among jazz fans, another California musician, Dave Brubeck, was writing modern jazz that appealed to a large mainstream audience.

Brubeck, born in 1920, was raised on Mozart, Bach, and Beethoven. His mother, a classical piano teacher, steered him toward a musical career. At college he listened to the experimental twentieth-century classical works of Arnold Schoenberg and studied music with French composer Darius Milhaud, who also wrote jazz.

In 1951 Brubeck formed the Dave Brubeck Quartet with alto saxophonist Paul Desmond, drummer Joe Dodge, and bassist Bob Bates. This group's sound epitomized the West Coast cool school with Brubeck's light touch on the piano matched by Desmond's lyrical style of improvisation. Shunning the rapid-fire style of beboppers, Desmond was known for his ability to pick a few sweet notes. As Brubeck remembers,

> There are so few guys that can play with the purity Paul had . . . people who can develop a theme and not play a million notes, but rather choice notes. . . . Paul was picking those notes with a great combination of intellect and concern for the purity of his sound and he wasn't out to dazzle anyone. [49]

Despite Brubeck's modest assessment, the Dave Brubeck Quartet did dazzle audiences—and these were not typical jazz crowds. The group avoided smoky, dark jazz clubs and instead booked gigs on college campuses, touring the country in Brubeck's station wagon with the string bass tied to the roof. At the time, playing schools was a controversial move. As Brubeck says, "Most [schools] in the United States still wouldn't let you play jazz, even in a practice room."[50] Nonetheless, the middle-class college students loved Brubeck's modern jazz sound.

In another bold move, Brubeck released a live album, *Jazz at Oberlin,* recorded at the Ohio college. When this, the first live jazz album, was released in 1953, it sold so well that the band was signed by the prestigious Columbia Records. When a second live album, *Jazz Goes to College,* was released in 1954, it sold over one hundred thousand copies, a huge number for that era. These record-setting sales gained the notice of *Time,* whose editors put Brubeck on the magazine's cover—making him

The Dave Brubeck Quartet, led by Brubeck on piano, found a new jazz audience among middle-class college students.

the first jazz musician to ever be so honored.

Throughout the fifties, the Dave Brubeck Quartet was the defining sound of West Coast jazz for most Americans. Yet Brubeck's group continued to innovate. For example, in 1959, the quartet released "Take Five," a song recorded in the 5/4 time signature as opposed to the standard 4/4. Despite its unusual rhythms, "Take Five" became the first jazz record in history to sell more than a million copies. The success of this innovative song inspired the Brubeck group to experiment with other unusual time signatures, such as 7/8 and 9/8.

Davis Grooves with Hard Bop

The music played by Brubeck and his contemporaries was not adopted by everyone. Although the laid-back West Coast cool jazz sold millions of records to suburban audiences, it "went largely unnoticed by [black] musicians in the East, except as an irritant,"[51] according to author Joe Goldberg. Instead, black jazz musicians in New York continued to push the boundaries with their music, playing a style known as hard bop for their own gratification rather than the approval of the "square" audiences that were attracted to Brubeck and others.

In contrast to cool jazz, hard bop is bebop taken to a higher level of complexity. Hard bop often has a hard-driving beat, blues-based improvisations, and passionate, complex solos. As Mark C. Gridley writes, "In

contrast to the polite, chamber music feeling projected by much of the West Coast style, *some* hard bop projected a funky, earthy feeling."[52]

Once again, Miles Davis led the way in the new style. With his 1954 recording of *Bags' Groove* with Kenny Clarke on drums, Thelonious Monk on piano, Horace Silver on bass and piano, Sonny Rollins on tenor sax, and Milt Jackson on vibraphone, Davis pioneered the postbebop sound that would come to be known as hard bop. The solos were brassy, the melodies were catchy, and the beat felt more like rhythm and blues than fast-paced bebop. John Edward Hasse describes how hard bop musicians achieved their sound,

> The hard-bop musicians used much the same vocabulary and grammar as bebop, but they turned the language to somewhat different ends to suit the demands of a new decade. They relaxed the tempos that had often made bebop a breathtaking steeplechase, and they simplified the knotty melodies that had delighted Parker and Dizzy Gillespie. In so doing, the hard-bop players brought back an earthy soulfulness that had receded during the boppers' quest for more "serious" recognition.
>
> This soulfulness had its roots in the ecstasy of church and gospel music, which provided the first listening experience for many black musicians, and which permeates such hard-bop classics.[53]

Art Blakey's energetic drumming was the driving force behind the Jazz Messengers.

The Messengers Deliver

Pianist and composer Silver, who played with Davis on *Bags' Groove* and other albums, went on to become a leading proponent of hard bop. Joining forces with drummer Art Blakey, Silver put together a quintet called the Jazz Messengers in 1955. The Messengers put a friendly face on hard bop, mixing improvised horn sounds, an infectious walking bass line, and Blakey's boisterous, rocking beat. Silver later described the band's attitude: "We weren't trying to do nothing but just cook, swing, make it happen. We called Art 'Little Dynamo,' he had so much drive, power, swing. . . . Art was loud—

robust, you know? . . . You had to match up so as not [to] sound like a weakling or a fool."[54]

The music of the Messengers appealed to listeners who could relate to the blues- and swing-driven sounds not found in bebop. After the release of the 1955 live album *At the Café Bohemia,* the Jazz Messengers' singles were blasting out of jukeboxes in African American neighborhoods coast to coast.

Over the decades, the Jazz Messengers would serve as a training ground for musicians who would go on to become stars in their own right, including trumpet players Donald Byrd, Freddie Hubbard, Chuck Mangione, Woody Shaw, and Wynton Marsalis; pianists Keith Jarrett and JoAnne Brackeen; and saxophonist Wayne Shorter. These musicians, in turn, formed their own bands and passed the stream of hard bop jazz down to the next generation.

Jazz Giant Coltrane

The sound of hard bop was defined by the rollicking drums, the brassy trumpet, and the earthy sound of the wailing tenor sax. And some of the greatest tenor sax players of the 1950s, including Sonny Rollins and Dexter Gordon, cut their chops on bebop and hard bop. Influenced by swing tenor players such as Coleman Hawkins and Lester Young, sax stars of the 1950s such as Gordon projected a rich, smoky tone while blowing long strings of riffs without taking a breath.

Art Blakey's Drum Style

As the leader of the Jazz Messengers for more than four decades, the drumming of Art Blakey is the rock-solid foundation of hard bop. Blakey's groundbreaking style is explored on the Public Broadcasting System's Jazz: A Film by Ken Burns *website:*

Although Blakey discourages comparison of his own music with African drumming, he adopted several African devices after his visit in 1948–9, including rapping on the side of the drum and using his elbow on the tom-tom to alter the pitch. Later he organized recording sessions with multiple drummers, including some African musicians and pieces. His much-imitated trademark, the forceful closing of the hi-hat on every second and fourth beat, has been part of his style since 1950–51.

Blakey is a major figure in modern jazz and an important stylist in drums. From his earliest recording sessions . . . particularly in his historic sessions with [Thelonious] Monk in 1947, he exudes power and originality, creating a dark cymbal sound punctuated by frequent loud snare and bass drum accents in triplets or cross-rhythms. A loud and domineering drummer, Blakey also listens and responds to his soloists. His contribution to jazz as a discoverer and molder of young talent over three decades is no less significant than his very considerable innovations on his instrument.

One of the many tenor players Gordon influenced went on to forever change the way the tenor saxophone was used. As editor Carl Woideck writes in *The John Coltrane Companion,*

John Coltrane's significance in jazz history—as a saxophonist, composer, and bandleader—is comparable only with a handful of other figures. His improvisational and compositional contributions were so broad that his music influenced players on all instruments, not just saxophone. More than thirty years after his death, young jazz musicians several generations removed from Coltrane are still inspired by his dedication to music, pursuit of musical knowledge, and pursuit of instrumental technique. [55]

Coltrane had played with Dizzy Gillespie during the late forties and early fifties, and he had been a member of the Miles Davis quintet between 1955 and 1957. Throughout much of this time Coltrane was a heroin addict, but he gave up drugs, alcohol, and even cigarettes in 1957 and began to study Eastern religions, meditation, and yoga. This spiritual awakening led him to study the music of India, particularly songs known as ragas, which are partly improvised scales, melodies, and rhyth-mic patterns that are intended to create different moods. Some are exciting, some deeply hypnotic. As Coltrane once said, "Most of what we play in jazz has the feeling of . . . raga."[56] And these songs, which combined technical skill, musical innovation, and a deep spiritual feel, strongly influenced his music for a time.

Like Davis, Coltrane's playing was always changing, never static. He was not afraid to experiment, pioneering such techniques as blowing several

After playing with such jazz greats as Dizzy Gillespie and Miles Davis, saxophonist John Coltrane (right) struck out on his own to become one of the most influential figures in jazz. Here he is accompanied by trumpeter Lee Morgan.

notes at once, bending his tones in a bluesy manner, and playing extended solos. These techniques, however, were controversial. One critic called Coltrane's music "anti-jazz"; however, critic Ira Gitler famously defined Coltrane's music as "sheets of sound."[57]

Coltrane's landmark solo albums, such as 1957's *Blue Trane,* 1958's *Soul Trane,* and 1960's *Giant Steps,* made Coltrane an international star. Meanwhile, Coltrane continued to record with Davis, Monk, and others. By the early sixties, the sax player was releasing an album a year. But it was his jazzed-up soprano saxophone version of the Rogers and Hammerstein song "My Favorite Things," from the hit musical play *The Sound of Music,* that brought Coltrane his biggest success in 1961.

This unlikely choice for groundbreaking jazz became Coltrane's signature tune. Weighing in at an astounding fourteen minutes (in an era when the average pop tune was under three minutes), the song allows the sax player to showcase his talents. Coltrane's fingers run up and down the keys as he dances around the melody, swooping and soaring, throwing in fluttering trills, and alternately making his horn sing, then screech, like a bird. And this jazzed-up version of a popular song brought Coltrane widespread notice from the general public, which might not have heard his music otherwise.

At the top of his form, Coltrane continued to release albums throughout the sixties, some experimenting with pop melodies, others taking off on the untrammeled musical paths with Indian ragas and free-form experimentation. The jazz world was stunned when the sax master died of liver cancer at the age of forty-one in 1967. But Coltrane had dozens of finished albums "in the can" that were gradually released for years after his death.

Although Coltrane has been identified as one of the most influential jazz artists of any age, few were able to follow in his footsteps. Nonetheless, he inspired musicians to take chances, devote themselves to their music, and continue to experiment in the face of criticism. But long after his death, Coltrane's music still sounds very alive, as Wynton Marsalis describes it in episode 9 of *Jazz: A Film by Ken Burns:*

> [The] thing that's always in John Coltrane is the lyrical shout of the preacher in the heat and full fury of attempting to transform the congregation. And that's the source of John Coltrane's power. We talk about sheets of sound . . . all the different things that he did. He . . . brought a lot of things into his music but the center of his music is that Sunday morning pulpit revival church meeting holler and shout. And more than any other jazz musician, he has that in his sound.[58]

Freedom Jazz

Although Coltrane played in a style all his own, some of his work has been identified as free jazz—chaotic music

Remembering Coltrane

John Coltrane was a legend in his own time. Writing for the online magazine Culture Kiosque, *jazz musician and critic Mike Zwerin offers his insight into the personality of the jazz giant:*

Coltrane . . . told [jazz pianist] Leonard Feather: "I never thought about whether or not people understand what I'm doing. The emotional reaction is all that matters. As long as there's some feeling of communication, it isn't necessary that it be understood."

By the time he died, his influence was pervasive. Other saxophonists figured that if Coltrane was playing tritones [three notes at a time], they'd better learn too. . . .

And by a generation later, his "funny" sound and striving articulation had become the standard stuff of the tenor saxophone. His harmonic innovations began to be analyzed in "Coltrane 101" [music] courses. . . .

His explosive combination of spiritual energy and intellectual prowess went beyond success and even beyond music into the metaphysical. He studied Eastern religions, Islam, the Torah. He read books about mathematics, personal improvement, van Gogh, African history and yoga. . . .

Improvisation was his vehicle for a search for self-knowledge, unity and the holy spirit. It led him to the Hindu concept of Om, which he defined as "the first vibration—that sound, that spirit which sets everything else into being."

The longer he played, the more you wanted to hear. Once after a 30-minute solo accompanied by the surging time of Elvin Jones, Mc-Coy Tyner's insistent chords and Jimme Garrison's muscular bass, Coltrane was driven to fall on his knees by the intensity of it all. A large baldheaded man wearing only a loin cloth ran up to the stage, raised his arms and shouted: "Coltrane!" The audience rose and shouted with him "Col-trane! Col-trane!" People kissed his hand as he walked out.

that sometimes sounds like musicians battling one another with riffs rather than playing together.

Free jazz evolved during the 1960s, when improvisation was liberated from traditional musical rules such as melody, rhythm, key, and preset chord progressions. This gives free jazz an anything-goes sort of rolling, tumbling sound, often described as turbulent and frenzied. A far different sound than anything ever imagined by Louis Armstrong and other jazz founders, free jazz is considered by some purists to be the ultimate in jazz expression.

Alto saxophonist Ornette Coleman and pianist Cecil Taylor are the founding fathers of the school of musical expression known as outside or free jazz. These musicians valued emotional expression over technical proficiency.

Coleman's work dispensed with melody, steady rhythm, and chord progressions in favor of wringing a wide array of unusual sounds from his instrument. As Gridley writes, Coleman "earned a reputation for more extensive manipulations of pitch and tone quality. . . . Ultra-high register playing [called altissimo], plus shrieks, squawks, wails, gurgles, and squeals were common. . . . Sustained notes alternated with screeches and moans."[59]

To obtain his sound, Coleman sometimes abandoned his brass saxophone and instead played a plastic toy sax that

One of the pioneers of free jazz, alto saxophonist Ornette Coleman introduced sounds not often heard in jazz music, such as shrieks, squawks and squeals.

emitted an unearthly screech. This innovation inspired other free jazz groups, such as the Art Ensemble of Chicago to search out other unusual noisemakers, including whistles, gongs, toy instruments, and bells.

By the midsixties Coleman had taught himself to play violin and trumpet, which he added to his free-flowing, formless jams. Meanwhile, Taylor and bassist Charles Mingus were coaxing a wide array of odd sounds from their instruments. Whereas Taylor's piano playing sounded like random skittering and pounding over the keys, Mingus invented a world of his own, described by Dirk Sutro in *Jazz for Dummies*:

> Seldom has a jazz musician combined such intricate songwriting with loose, inspired performances by all the players. Raw, squealing horns skitter over Mingus's low, rumbling bass and seem to capture the energy and uncertainty of [the 1960s, an] era of rapid change in America. . . .
>
> The album *Mingus Mingus Mingus Mingus Mingus* . . . from 1963 opens with Mingus's bass calling out in a deep, moaning voice. Here again, and throughout this collection, are Mingus's dense,

dark arrangements of horns; his playing is extremely assured as he drives his band relentlessly with a thrumming undercurrent. . . . Mingus's guttural hog call opens "Hog Callin' Blues" on his 1962 album *Oh Yeah*. . . . Mingus is at his grittiest best on this session, which includes plenty of bass playing, but also his shouts and groans as he gooses a band.[60]

Inspiration for a New Generation

The 1950s and 1960s were a golden age of jazz when cool, hard, and free styles changed the vocabulary of music and inspired experimental composition in other styles, from classical music to rock. The free jazz shrieks emanating from Ornette Coleman's horn inspired the howling lead guitar of rock and roller Jimi Hendrix later in the decade. Coltrane's unique, soulful improvisations provided musical insight to everyone from classical composer Leonard Bernstein to rock musician Beck. And the sounds of the cool, the hard, and the free would also inspire the next wave of jazz players, who would fuse rock, classical, and jazz into a new sound—and a new expression for a new generation.

Chapter Six

Fusion and Beyond

The second half of the 1960s was a time of unbridled experimentation in all styles of music. And it was an era when bands incorporated dozens of different instruments and musical styles into their songs. Traditional classical instruments such as cellos, flutes, oboes, and French horns were used as accompaniments by rock groups such as the Beatles, while bands like Blood, Sweat, and Tears recorded a type of rock-jazz fusion using saxophones, trumpets, congas, and trombones. Rock groups such as the Grateful Dead with Jerry Garcia, and Cream, featuring Eric Clapton, popularized jazzlike jamming in which long, improvised guitar solos were melded with wild bass riffs and African-style polyrhythmic drumming. And relatively new instruments, such as electric pianos, organs, and synthesizers, joined the ever-advancing technology of electric guitars, amplifiers, and sound effect pedals such as the wa-wa, fuzz tone, and phase shifter.

By the time John Coltrane died in 1967, the music business was almost totally dominated by the new sounds of soul and rock and roll. The brave and bold jazz experimentation by 1950s-era players sounded almost quaint in comparison to the psychedelic cacophony of the late 1960s. As Peter Keepnews writes in *The Oxford Companion to Jazz,*

Listeners who a few years earlier might have gravitated toward jazz had by the late sixties discovered in the music of the Beatles, Bob Dylan, Jimi Hendrix, and others not just the [primitive] excitement that had always been at the heart of rock-and-roll but also a considerable degree of musical sophistication—as well as lyrics that, in one way or another, addressed the growing, if vaguely defined, sense that the old social and political order was crumbling and some sort of utopian revolution was in the air. It was hard for jazz, a primarily instrumental music with roots stretching back to the early days of the century, to compete with a music that literally spoke to its listeners about the concerns and emotions of the moment. [61]

To add to its problems, jazz was divided against itself. Traditional players believed that the squeaking, honking sound of free jazz did not even deserve to be called jazz, and that such musical experimentation alienated the traditional audience for the genre. Many jazz musicians who had been famous in earlier decades struggled along, playing one-night stands in small clubs; others moved to Europe, where hard bop, cool jazz, and free jazz were still appreciated by large audiences. But in America, according to Miles Davis, "All of a sudden jazz became passé, something dead you put under a glass in the museum and study. All of a sudden rock 'n' roll was in the forefront of the media." [62]

Jazz Meets Rock

Against this backdrop of discord within the jazz community, a new generation of jazz artists decided that rather than

Rock groups like the Grateful Dead borrowed the improvisational style of jazz bands. Their concerts featured long guitar solos combined with wild bass riffs.

fight the rock tidal wave, they would join it by incorporating the most commercially successful elements of rock and roll into jazz music. And a new form of jazz, called fusion, emerged from this meeting of musical genres.

Fusion musicians tended to favor electric guitars, pianos, organs, and synthesizers over the traditional saxophone and trumpet configurations of earlier jazz combos. The stand-up bass was replaced by the electric bass guitar. Drummers expanded their kits, adding bells, shakers, rattles, and other traditional Latin and African percussion instruments. And the drummers shunned the stretched and broken rhythms of free jazz in favor of the straight-ahead 4/4 rock beat.

With all of these electronic instruments and drums, the new jazz was loud—much louder than that played with horns and string basses. Yet the musicians who made this jazz were relying on a deep knowledge of music as well. As Bill Milkowski writes in *The Oxford Companion to Jazz,*

> Volume was a key component of the early fusion movement and part of the new vocabulary that jazzers were becoming acquainted with. Propelled by sheer decibels and a blistering intensity, this adventurous new music was tempered by a sophisticated sense of harmony and theory that went well beyond the scope of most rock musicians of the day.[63]

The new sound of fusion was rejected by many jazz traditionalists, who called it "con-fusion,"[64] but it caught the ears of the younger generation, who had grown up with rock and roll. As innovative jazz guitarist Larry Coryell recalled,

> We were in the middle of a world cultural revolution. Everybody was dropping acid [LSD] and the prevailing attitude was "Let's do something different." We loved [jazz guitarist Wes Montgomery] but we also loved Bob Dylan. We loved Coltrane but we also dug the Beatles. We loved Miles [Davis] but we also loved the Rolling Stones.[65]

In addition to influencing the music, rock and roll even changed the look of jazz. The colorful clothing and long hair sported by rock stars was adopted by fusion musicians as well. And with drugs such as LSD replacing heroin, even in the jazz community the music developed a psychedelic edge where jams tended toward the expansive and "spacey."

Davis Brews a New Sound

Some old faces could still be found on the fusion scene, however. Miles Davis had been inventing new jazz styles for nearly his entire career, pioneering cool jazz and hard bop during the 1950s. So it was no surprise that the man who had pronounced jazz passé was able to single-handedly jump-start the fusion era in 1969 with the album *Bitches Brew.*

To record the album, Davis filled the studio with musicians who would later become a who's who of mass-market

Jazz Influence on Rock Musicians

Although rock music influenced jazz during the 1960s, jazz influenced rock groups such as the Mothers of Invention, led by Frank Zappa, as Bill Milkowski writes in The Oxford Companion to Jazz:

Frank Zappa's contribution to [the] cross-fertilization process that was occurring between rock and jazz in 1966 cannot be overstated. On his first album—the highly experimental underground classic—*Freak Out!* . . .Zappa listed the names of jazz greats Cecil Taylor, Roland Kirk, Eric Dolphy, and Charles Mingus . . . as important influences on his music. . . .

The year 1967 was pivotal for the courtship of rock and jazz. In its July issue that year, the staunch jazz publication *Down Beat* announced that it would expand its coverage to encompass rock. . . . Jimi Hendrix melded electronic feedback to Mitch Mitchell's swinging ride cymbal work on "Third Stone from the Sun," arguably Jimi's "jazziest" tune and a centerpiece on his . . . debut, *Are You Experienced?* Earlier that year, Hendrix had jammed with [jazz horn master] Rahsaan Roland Kirk at Ronnie Scott's nightclub in London. Back in the States, [Byrds' leader] Roger McGuinn had John Coltrane's "sheets of sound" in mind when he recorded his droning guitar parts to the Byrds' [number-one hit] "Eight Miles High," while Lou Reed had Ornette Coleman in mind when he cut his avant-punk guitar solo to "I Heard Her Call My Name" from the Velvet Undergound's *White Light/White Heat*. . . . Detroit's notorious proto-punk band MC5 began using feedback as a musical tool and loudness as an aesthetic unit in its long, extended improvisations inspired by the avant-garde jazz movement.

jazz fusion, including drummers Don Alias, Lenny White, and Jack De-Johnette; percussionists Airto Moreira and Jim Riley; electric bassists Harvey Brooks and Dave Holland; saxophonist Wayne Shorter; electric guitarist John McLaughlin; and pianists Chick Corea and Joe Zawinul.

The original recording of *Bitches Brew* was a double record set with only seven songs on four sides of vinyl. The title track clocked in at more than

Miles Davis (center) assembled a prestigious group of jazz musicians that included bassist Dave Holland and keyboard player Chick Corea to record the album Bitches Brew.

twenty-six minutes, and at any given time up to twelve musicians might be jamming at once.

The sound itself is a collection of musical phrases tossed out by the individual players rather than the traditional jazz style of musicians trading solos. And the electric keyboards and guitars give the music the sound of a rock band jamming. Some tracks exude a slow, textured, hypnotic, psychedelic sound while others feature rock riffing with McLaughlin's solid guitar chords in counterpoint to piano runs. Davis often maintains his trademark moody

tone, but at times his chaotic riffs seemed more inspired by the howling guitar runs of rock star Jimi Hendrix than the smooth bop melodies of Dizzy Gillespie.

Bitches Brew was a stunning success, with fans of three musical styles, rock, jazz, and blues, pushing the sales figures toward a million. Davis spent the next six years recording enough material for twenty albums, twelve of which were released. During this era, the trumpet wizard continued to forge a rock-solid fusion sound, with each successive album covering new musical ground. Some albums, such as the 1972 movie soundtrack *A Tribute to Jack Johnson,* are almost straight-ahead rockers. Meanwhile, the album *On the Corner,* released the same year, pays tribute to the grooving funk beat, with Davis playing his horn, enhanced at times through the use of a wa-wa pedal.

By 1975 Davis had been on the road nearly nonstop for more than thirty years. Burned out from the constant travel from one concert to another, the jazz innovator retired, later claiming that he had not touched his trumpet once for five full years. By the time he reappeared on the music scene in 1980, the fusion style he had spawned was being played by dozens of groups and had become one of the biggest commercial success stories in jazz history since the swing era.

McLaughlin's *Birds of Fire*

Bitches Brew got much of its unique fusion sound from the playing of British guitar wizard John McLaughlin. With the debut of the album *Birds of Fire,* McLaughlin changed the meaning of jazz guitar while also exerting great influence on hundreds of rock guitarists, as Mark C. Gridley writes:

McLaughlin is notable for a phenomenally high level of instrumental proficiency. . . . He may also be responsible for some of the rise in musicianship which has characterized rock guitarists since 1970. Despite his being considered a jazz musician, McLaughlin used a tone which was unlike traditional jazz guitar quality [heard in earlier decades]. It was hard, not soft, cutting, not smooth, and metallic, not warm. In short, it had the color and texture preferred by rock guitarists, not jazz guitarists. And he frequently altered the size and shape of his tone by use of a wah wah pedal and phase shifter. (The phase shifter produces a subtle swirling of the sound.) Another point of contrast between McLaughlin and the jazz tradition is that most of McLaughlin's improvisations contain far less of the . . . easy, relaxed, swing feeling that had previously typified jazz.[66]

McLaughlin formed his own band, the Mahavishnu Orchestra, in 1971. (The band's name was suggested by McLaughlin's Indian spiritual adviser, Sri Chimnoy. *Mahavishnu* means "divine compassion, power, and justice" in Hindi.) The unique records of the Mahavishnu Orchestra, which combined rock, Indian raga, and jazz, sold phenomenally well. And the band toured the world nearly nonstop in the early seventies, playing to sold-out crowds everywhere. The pressures of fame, however, proved to be too much for McLaughlin, who broke up the band in 1975. The guitarist would continue to record with other jazz and Indian musicians in the decades that followed, however.

Pat Metheny's Boundless Imagination

As might be expected, the fusion of jazz and rock and roll opened the door to a wide array of individual interpretations of what the new style entailed. Like McLaughlin, Missouri-born Pat Metheny had his own unique musical voice that allowed him to become a commercial success during the 1970s.

Guitarist Pat Metheny became one of the foremost performers of music that fused jazz and rock 'n' roll.

Metheny was a musical prodigy who began teaching at the prestigious Berklee College of Music in Boston while still in his teens. At twenty-three he started a band with pianist Lyle Mays, and by the 1980s the albums of the Pat Metheny Group, such as *American Garage* and *Off Ramp,* were best-sellers, consistently moving one hundred thousand copies or more. By 1985 Metheny had recorded a dozen albums in a nine-year period, three of them receiving nominations for the Grammy Award, which is one of the highest honors a musician can receive for recorded music.

With its easygoing sound fueled by the phase shifter effect on the electric guitar, Metheny's music has been described as folk-jazz, easy-listening jazz, or simply mood music. And as one of fusion's eminent performers, Metheny has also produced and recorded with dozens of jazz legends, including Ornette Coleman, Jack DeJohnette, Sonny Rollins, and Miles Davis. These musicians, in turn, have influenced Metheny's guitar compositions. As Calvin Wilson writes in *Jazz: The First Century,*

> Metheny, more than many others, symbolized the flexibility of late [twentieth-] century jazz. In a typical performance, his group drew from bop, Brazilian samba, even the most out-and-out avant-garde jazz, employing virtually any stylistic and sonic element as long as it supported the musical statement being made. . . .

Moreira Shakes the Dance Floors

Brazilian-born Airto Moreira is one of the most renowned percussionists in jazz. His use of traditional drums, rattles, and percussive sound effects from his native land have influenced jazz, rock, and fusion. His official website, Airto.com, contains the following information about the drummer:

Airto Moreira was born in 1941 in the small village of Itaiopolis south Brazil, and was raised in Curitiba. Even before he could walk he would start shaking and banging on the floor every time the radio played a hot song. This worried his mother, but his grandmother recognized his potential and encouraged him to express himself. . . . At thirteen he became a professional musician, playing percussion, drums, and singing in local dance bands. . . .

His vocals, drumming and unique percussion style has attracted an audience interested in world music, jazz, and the new dance music movement. . . . His impact was so powerful that *Down Beat* magazine added the category of percussion to its readers' and critics' polls, which he has won over twenty times since 1973. In the past few years he was voted number one percussionist by *Jazz Times, Modern Drummer,* and *Jazz Izz* magazine, as well as in many European, Latin American and Asian publications. Lately Airto has won *Drum Magazine* readers' poll and Jazz Central Station's Global Jazz Poll on the Internet. Most recently Airto performed as a guest star with the Boston Pops Philharmonic Orchestra on a special for the PBS TV, the Smashing Pumpkins' "Unplugged" for MTV, the Japan-based percussion group Kodo and Depeche Mode's latest CD "Exciter." . . .

Airto's latest album entitled "Homeless," which was released in the year 2000 by the British label Electric Melt is a high-energy album with "tribal" rhythms that is shaking the dance floors around the world.

Metheny proved an improviser of boundless imagination and energy. He also proved one of the most commercially successful jazz musicians of the 1980s, just as the fusion movement reached a larger audience than had the mainstream jazz of preceding years. [67]

Chick Corea

Keyboardist Chick Corea was another *Bitches Brew* alumnus who took fusion to another level both musically and in the marketplace. Thanks to his work recording and touring with Davis, Corea, born in Massachusetts in 1941, was an international star by the early 1970s. In 1972 he formed a band called Return to Forever with saxophonist Joe Farrell, respected jazz bassist Stanley Clarke, Brazilian percussionist Airto Moreira (another Davis alumnus), and Moreira's wife, vocalist Flora Purim. The albums *Return to Forever* and *Light as a Feather* have a unique sound, strongly influenced by the samba-flavored beat of Moreira and the soaring vocals of Purim, whose voice has a six-octave range.

While winning jazz polls year after year, Return to Forever recorded throughout the seventies despite constant personnel changes. Corea continued to record as a solo artist, experimenting with electronic ensembles, solo piano, classical music, and high-powered acoustic duos. Several of the pianist's compositions, such as "Spain," "La Fiesta," and "Windows," have become jazz standards.

The Jazz Fusion Weather Report

Joe Zawinul, another keyboard player who jammed with Miles Davis on *Bitches Brew,* was responsible for founding the group Weather Report with other Davis alumni such as Shorter and Moreira. With this stellar lineup, Weather Report was one of the premier jazz-fusion supergroups of the last three decades of the twentieth century. The music created by these men is a lively mix of Latin samba, African dance rhythms, beat-heavy funk, rock, and jazz improvisation. Like many other jazz groups, members of Weather Report often bounced back and forth between other groups or recorded fusion records under their own names. As the personnel changed, so did the sound of the band.

By 1976 renowned bassist Jaco Pastorius had joined the band (after several years with Metheny), and his melodious, phase-shifting bass guitar runs inspired a generation of bass players, as Wilson explains:

> A phenomenal technician with a boundless musical imagination, Pastorius was as capable of firing off rapid, precisely articulated bop phrases as he was of coaxing plaintive, voicelike melodies from his distinctive instrument of choice, a fretless electric bass. He spawned an army of imitators and drew raves as the instrument's most influential practitioner. [68]

During the Pastorius era, Weather Report reached its peak of fame, bringing freewheeling jam sessions to concert stages across the globe. In 1977 the album *Heavy Weather* became a best-seller, and its song "Birdland" became an instant jazz standard.

Herbie Hancock's *Headhunters*

Although Zawinul had only begun playing with Davis in 1969, Chicago pianist Herbie Hancock had been jamming with the trumpet player since 1963. And during the sixties, Hancock wrote and recorded dozens of jazz standards, including "The Sorcerer," "Cantaloupe Island," and "Riot."

In 1973 Hancock recorded his masterpiece *Headhunters,* a heavily electric jazz fusion record that quickly went on to become the best-selling jazz album in history. The lead song on the album, "Chameleon," fuses funk and jazz, sounding more like the funk master James Brown than jazz rock.

Headhunters made Hancock an international superstar, and he continued

Herbie Hancock's Headhunters *became the best-selling jazz album of all time and transformed the pianist into an international superstar.*

to record best-selling albums. In 1981 he teamed up with Corea and pianists Keith Jarrett and McCoy Tyner on the album *Corea/Hancock/Jarrett/Tyner,* a musical feast for lovers of acoustic jazz piano.

Hancock continued to record throughout the following decades. In 1995 he further blurred the lines between rock and jazz on his album *New Standard* when he recorded fusion versions of songs by rock legends Prince, the Beatles, Stevie Wonder, and even the grunge band Nirvana.

Marsalis's Postbop

In 1981 Hancock played the Newport Jazz Festival backed by a young trumpet player named Wynton Marsalis, who quickly became an international superstar in his own right, playing a new style called neo-bop, or postbop, based on the bop and hard bop of an earlier generation. Although hard to define, postbop is a sort of fusion of all jazz styles, and it can incorporate blues as well. As Scott Yanow writes on the ARTISTdirect Network website,

It has become increasingly difficult to categorize modern jazz. A large segment of the music does not fit into any historical style, is not as rock-oriented as fusion or as free as [free jazz]. Starting with the rise of [trumpet player] Wynton Marsalis in 1979, a whole generation of younger players chose to play an updated variety of hard bop that was also influenced by the mid-1960's Miles Davis Quintet and aspects of free jazz. Since this music (which often features complex chordal improvisation) has become the norm for jazz in the 1990's, the terms "Modern Mainstream" or "Post Bop" . . . symbolize the eclectic scene as jazz enters its second century. [69]

As a founder of the postbop movement, Marsalis toured with Art Blakey's Jazz Messengers when only nineteen years old. In 1981 he released *Wynton Marsalis,* his debut album as a jazz bandleader. The album's success helped increase the popularity of jazz music among a younger audience.

Over the years Marsalis has recorded in many jazz styles, from old-style New Orleans to bop to cool jazz. His albums are sometimes reminiscent of Davis and Coltrane during the 1960s, and at other times they recall the elegance of Duke Ellington.

Marsalis's contributions to jazz have been more than musical. He has also dedicated his life to promoting jazz as a respectable art form while keeping the style alive by bringing the music to a younger audience. To do this, Marsalis places a premium on teaching. As a leading jazz ambassador among young people, Marsalis was a welcome addition at the Lincoln Center Jazz for Young People program in New York. And while touring the country, Marsalis often meets with students to conduct master classes in jazz music

In addition to his extensive musical contributions as a performer, Wynton Marsalis has helped popularize jazz with younger audiences by meeting with students across the country.

and trumpet playing. In 1996 Marsalis won the prestigious Peabody Award for his twenty-six-part series "Marsalis on Music" heard on National Public Radio. In keeping with his goal of educating the public about jazz, Marsalis acted as the senior creative consultant on *Jazz: A Film by Ken Burns,* which appeared on the Public Broadcasting Service in 2001.

Neo-Bop to Hip Hop

Jazz has continued to evolve as artists incorporate elements of other musical styles. The success of Marsalis created a demand for other so-called young lions of post-bop, such as trumpeter Nicholas Payne and pianist Marcus Roberts. But the return to bop did not appeal to other musicians of the 1990s, such as those in the group M-Base, whose new music incorporated the sounds of rock, hip hop, soul, and funk into a street-smart blend of jazz-rap rhythms. (*M-Base* is an acronym for "Macro-Basic Array of Structured Extemporization.")

The founder of M-Base, alto sax player Steve Coleman, grew up listening to Charlie Parker. He recorded half a dozen albums with M-Base during the 1990s that had an ever-changing array of musicians, including tenor saxophonist Gary Thomas, pianist Geri Allen, and renowned jazz singer Cassandra Wilson.

The experimental sound of M-Base inspired the next generation of musicians, whose unfettered approach to experimental jazz combines musical talent with the most up-to-date studio techniques, such as digital sampling, which involves incorporating prerecorded digitized snippets, or "samples," of music.

The band Digable Planets is a good example of a group that combines hip hop with jazz while sampling Art Blakey, Sonny Rollins, and Curtis Mayfield. On their 1993 album *Reachin' (A New Refutation of Time and Space)*, the lyrics and beat are rap and the music has a laid-back, jazzy groove. Other groups that mix rap lyrics with jazz jamming include A Tribe Called Quest, the Roots, and Gang Star.

The 1990s Swing Revival

Whereas some bands infuse traditional jazz with modern musical styles, others have found their groove by reviving the old styles, polishing them up, and making them sound new again. Swing music, which fell out of fashion after World War II, was revived during the mid-1990s by a host of bands that mixed tongue-in-cheek humor with serious musical ability.

One of the first bands to capitalize on the swing revival was the Squirrel Nut Zippers, who play mostly their own compositions written in authentic old-time jazz style, mixing 1920s-era New Orleans jazz with the sounds of 1930s big-band swing and 1940s Latin-flavored rhythms.

Brian Setzer is probably the most well known of the swing revivalists, having achieved commercial success with the rockabilly band Stray Cats. Setzer mixes the big-band swing sound of Louis Prima and Count Basie with jazzed up treatments of rock-and-roll classics and originals.

Another band participating in the swing revival is the eight-piece Big Bad Voodoo Daddy, whose original compositions sound as if they were recorded during the 1940s.

Although the numbers of groups that have the talent and commercial savvy to revive swing are few, their success shows that the music of the twenties, thirties, and forties remains as powerful a force as it was more than half a century ago.

Steve Coleman founded M-Base, a band that inspired a new generation of musicians to experiment with combining jazz with other styles, such as hip hop, soul, and funk.

The Second Century of Jazz

As jazz moves into its second century, the music, in all of its various forms, remains alive and vital for its fans. Although not as popular as rock and country music in the United States, jazz is well loved around the world, and nations such as Great Britain, Denmark, Italy, and Japan have burgeoning jazz scenes. In fact, Japan, with only half as many people buys more jazz records than the United States does. And American jazz players have found that they can better expand their fan base by touring Europe and the Far East.

Even though jazz records only make up 4 to 5 percent of all CD sales worldwide, the music is acknowledged as an integral part of American culture and history. Even today the music of Armstrong, Goodman, Gillespie, Parker, Davis, Mingus, and others remains vital and timeless. Recordings of rock from the 1950s may sound old and dated, but Coltrane's saxophone blasts out of that era and continues to define "cool" even in the twenty-first century.

The musical style first played by Buddy Bolden during the 1890s has traveled a long and illustrious path, and its impact upon twentieth-century American music is undisputed. And with albums such as Miles Davis's 1959 *Kind of Blue* still selling more than 250,000 copies a year, there is little doubt that the sounds of jazz will continue to resonate for generations to come.

• Notes •

Introduction: "Never Played the Same Way Once"

1. Quoted in Dirk Sutro, *Jazz for Dummies*. Foster City, CA: IDG Books Worldwide, 1998, p. 8.
2. Quoted in Public Broadcasting Service, "Classroom," *Jazz: A Film by Ken Burns*. www.pbs.org.
3. Quoted in John Edward Hasse, ed., *Jazz: The First Century*. New York: William Morrow, 2000, p. iv.
4. Quoted in Hasse, *Jazz*, p. v.

Chapter One: The Roots of Jazz

5. Quoted in Hasse, *Jazz*, p. 5.
6. Mark C. Gridley, *Jazz Styles: History and Analysis*. Englewood Cliffs, NJ: Prentice-Hall, 1988, p. 40.
7. Donald D. Megill and Richard S. Demory, *Introduction to Jazz History*. New York: Prentice-Hall, 1993, p. 5.
8. Quoted in Alyn Shipton, *A New History of Jazz*. New York: Continuum, 2001, pp. 62–63.
9. Quoted in Shipton, *A New History of Jazz*, p. 84.
10. Hasse, *Jazz*, p. 16.
11. Shipton, *A New History of Jazz*, p. 82.
12. Quoted in Hasse, *Jazz*, p. 17.
13. Quoted in Hasse, *Jazz*, p. 18.
14. Quoted in Shipton, *A New History of Jazz*, p. 92.
15. Quoted in Shipton, *A New History of Jazz*, p. 96.
16. Quoted in Shipton, *A New History of Jazz*. p. 104.

Chapter Two: The Swingin' Jazz Age

17. Quoted in Hasse, *Jazz*, p. 26.
18. Quoted in George E. Mowry, *The Twenties: Fords, Flappers, and Fanatics*. Englewood Cliffs, NJ: Prentice-Hall, 1963, p. 66.
19. Richard Hadlock, *Jazz Masters of the 20's*. New York: Macmillan, 1965, p. 14.
20. Quoted in Hasse, *Jazz*, p. 31.
21. Quoted in Shipton, *A New History of Jazz*, p. 118.
22. Quoted in Hasse, *Jazz*, p. 28.
23. Shipton, *A New History of Jazz*, p. 138.
24. Quoted in Geoffrey C. Ward, *Jazz: A Film by Ken Burns*, episode 2, "The Gift," Florentine Films, 2000.
25. Gridley, *Jazz Styles*, p. 66.
26. Edward Kennedy "Duke" Ellington, *Music Is My Mistress*. Garden City, NY: Doubleday, 1973, p. 106.
27. Shipton, *A New History of Jazz*, p. 266.
28. Quoted in Shipton, *A New History of Jazz*, p. 267.

Chapter Three: Dancing to Swing

29. Quoted in Ward, *Jazz: A Film by Ken Burns,* episode 4, "The True Welcome."
30. Hasse, *Jazz,* p. 54.
31. Quoted in Ward, *Jazz: A Film by Ken Burns,* episode 4, "The True Welcome."
32. Quoted in Ward, *Jazz: A Film by Ken Burns,* episode 4, "The True Welcome."
33. Quoted in Shipton, *A New History of Jazz,* p. 308.
34. Quoted in Shipton, *A New History of Jazz,* p. 325.
35. Hasse, *Jazz,* p. 52.

Chapter Four: The Birth of Bebop

36. Quoted in Kenny Mathieson, *Giant Steps: Bebop and the Creators of Modern Jazz, 1945–65.* Edinburgh, UK: Payback, 1999, p. 7.
37. Quoted in Scott DeVeaux, *The Birth of Bebop: A Social and Musical History.* Berkeley and Los Angeles: University of California Press, 1997, p. 218.
38. Quoted in Shipton, *A New History of Jazz,* p. 444.
39. Gridley, *Jazz Styles,* pp. 152–53.
40. Dizzy Gillespie with Al Fraser, *To Be or Not to Bop.* Garden City, NY: Doubleday, 1979, p. 318.
41. Quoted in Ward, *Jazz: A Film by Ken Burns,* episode 8, "Risk."
42. Mathieson, *Giant Steps,* p. 160.
43. Quoted in Shipton, *A New History of Jazz,* p. 484.

44. Quoted in DeVeaux, *The Birth of Bebop,* p. 222.

Chapter Five: The Cool, the Hard, and the Free

45. Quoted in Ward, *Jazz: A Film by Ken Burns,* episode 8, "Risk."
46. Quoted in Don Crowson, "Miles Davis—A Life Story," February 2, 1998. www.nettally.com.
47. Geoffrey C. Ward, *Jazz: A History of America's Music.* New York: Alfred A. Knopf, 2000, p. 375.
48. Quoted in Alyn Shipton, *A New History of Jazz,* p. 701.
49. Quoted in Shipton, *A New History of Jazz,* p. 702.
50. Quoted in Ward, *Jazz: A History of America's Music,* p. 378.
51. Quoted in Hasse, *Jazz,* p. 115.
52. Gridley, *Jazz Styles,* p. 191.
53. Hasse, *Jazz,* p. 116.
54. Quoted in Shipton, *A New History of Jazz,* p. 673.
55. Carl Woideck, ed., *The John Coltrane Companion.* New York: Schirmer Books, 1998, p. xiii.
56. Quoted in Woideck, *The John Coltrane Companion,* p. 34.
57. Quoted in Shipton, *A New History of Jazz,* p. 746.
58. Quoted in Ward, *Jazz: A Film by Ken Burns,* episode 9, "The Adventure."
59. Gridley, *Jazz Styles,* p. 227.
60. Sutro, *Jazz for Dummies,* pp. 243–44.

Chapter Six: Fusion and Beyond

61. Quoted in Bill Kirchner, ed., *The Oxford Companion to Jazz.* Oxford,

UK: Oxford University Press, 2000, p. 489.

62. Quoted in Shipton, *A New History of Jazz,* p. 856.
63. Quoted in Kirchner, *The Oxford Companion to Jazz,* p. 505.
64. Quoted in Kirchner, *The Oxford Companion to Jazz,* p. 502.
65. Quoted in Kirchner, *The Oxford Companion to Jazz,* p. 503.
66. Gridley, *Jazz Styles,* p. 326.
67. Quoted in Hasse, *Jazz,* p. 198.
68. Quoted in Hasse, *Jazz,* p. 200.
69. Scott Yanow, "Music Genres: Post-Bop: History." http://genres.artist direct.com.

• For Further Reading •

George Crisp, *Miles Davis.* New York: Franklin Watts, 1997. A biography of the legendary jazz trumpeter who is responsible for the invention of several jazz styles, including hard bop and fusion.

Tony Gentry, *Dizzy Gillespie.* New York: Chelsea House, 1991. The life story of "the ambassador of jazz" who introduced the world to bebop.

Leslie Gourse, *Fancy Fretwork: The Great Jazz Guitarists.* New York: Franklin Watts, 1999. This book traces the evolution of the guitar in jazz music and offers biographical information about the world's greatest jazz guitarists from the early 1900s to the present.

———, *Striders to Beboppers and Beyond: The Art of Jazz Piano.* New York: Franklin Watts, 1997. This work explores the lives and music of some of the greatest jazz pianists and investigates their impact on the development of jazz music.

———, *Wynton Marsalis: Trumpet Genius.* New York: Franklin Watts, 1999. A discussion of the influences and musical career of the respected trumpet player renown for his performance of jazz and classical music.

James Haskins, *Black Music in America: A History Through Its People.* New York: HarperTrophy, 1993. This book follows the history of black music in America, from early slave songs to jazz and blues to soul and current trends.

Langston Hughes, *First Book of Jazz.* New York: Franklin Watts, 1982. An introduction to jazz, focusing on its historical development and famous performers, written by one of America's most respected black authors.

Stanley L. Mour, *American Jazz Musicians.* Springfield, NJ: Enslow, 1998. The biographies of ten renowned jazz musicians, including Louis Armstrong, John Coltrane, and Miles Davis, are provided in this book.

Christopher Raschka, *Charlie Parker Played Be Bop.* New York: Orchard Books, 1992. The tragic life story of one of jazz's most gifted saxophonists.

John W. Selfridge, *John Coltrane: A Sound Supreme.* New York: Franklin Watts, 1999. The author traces the life of the innovative jazz sax player and the evolution of his music.

Gene Seymour, *Jazz: The Great American Art.* New York: Franklin Watts, 1995. A history of jazz, from its roots in blues, ragtime, and swing.

Adam Woog, *Duke Ellington.* San Diego: Lucent Books, 1996. An in-depth exploration of the king of jazz with reflections on his life, music, and influence.

———, *Louis Armstrong.* San Diego: Lucent Books, 1995. A well-written biography of the most creative and influential musician the jazz world has ever known.

• Works Consulted •

Books

Bill Crow, *Jazz Anecdotes*. New York: Oxford University Press, 1990. This book offers more than three hundred pages of jokes, comments, commentary, and observations by the world's most respected jazz musicians about jazz music and the jazz scene.

Miles Davis with Quincy Troupe, *Miles: The Autobiography*. New York: Simon and Schuster, 1990. The triumphs, struggles, and canny observations of an enduring jazz legend.

Scott DeVeaux, *The Birth of Bebop: A Social and Musical History*. Berkeley and Los Angeles: University of California Press, 1997. The author discusses the development of "modern jazz," with recollections from its innovators and rich details of the pre–civil rights African American social scene.

Edward Kennedy "Duke" Ellington, *Music Is My Mistress*. Garden City, NY: Doubleday, 1973. The autobiography of a jazz music legend, filled with insightful anecdotes from a career that spanned more than five decades.

Dizzy Gillespie with Al Fraser, *To Be or Not to Bop*. Garden City, NY: Doubleday, 1979. The autobiography of the inventor of bebop, with humorous stories and astute observations.

Mark C. Gridley, *Jazz Styles: History and Analysis*. Englewood Cliffs, NJ: Prentice-Hall, 1988. A scholarly study of jazz with a detailed investigation of the musical techniques and cultural influences on the style.

Richard Hadlock, *Jazz Masters of the 20's*. New York: Macmillan, 1965. A book in the Macmillan Jazz Master series, this one explores jazz music during the Roaring Twenties.

Mickey Hart with Jay Stevens, *Drumming at the Edge of Magic*. San Francisco: HarperCollins, 1990. The compelling story of percussion, drums, and drumming from the man who played drums for the Grateful Dead for more than 30 years.

John Edward Hasse, ed., *Jazz: The First Century*. New York: William Morrow, 2000. This large, colorful book is filled with essays by widely respected authorities on jazz as well as interesting graphics and dozens of photographs.

Bill Kirchner, ed., *The Oxford Companion to Jazz*. Oxford, UK: Oxford University Press, 2000. A large and exhaustive summary of jazz history with chapters written by jazz scholars, performers, and critics on topics ranging from the African roots of the music to jazz clubs and dance.

Kenny Mathieson, *Giant Steps: Bebop and the Creators of Modern Jazz, 1945–65.* Edinburgh, UK: Payback, 1999. This book discusses the development of bebop and modern jazz between 1945 and 1965 as told through the life stories of players such as Dizzy Gillespie, Charlie Parker, Miles Davis, Max Roach, and others.

Donald D. Megill and Richard S. Demory, *Introduction to Jazz History.* New York: Prentice-Hall, 1993. An examination of jazz history from its African roots to the present.

George E. Mowry, *The Twenties: Fords, Flappers, and Fanatics.* Englewood Cliffs, NJ: Prentice-Hall, 1963. A colorful reading on the history of the Jazz Age in the United States.

Alyn Shipton, *A New History of Jazz.* New York: Continuum, 2001. An up-to-date examination of jazz history that brings new information and insight to the topic.

Dirk Sutro, *Jazz for Dummies.* Foster City, CA: IDG Books Worldwide, 1998. An amusing and easy-to-read exploration of jazz music, history, instruments, and players.

Geoffrey C. Ward, *Jazz: A History of America's Music.* New York: Alfred A. Knopf, 2000. One of the more comprehensive histories of jazz available, with enlightening text, interesting sidebars, and hundreds of vintage photos.

Carl Woideck, ed., *The John Coltrane Companion.* New York: Schirmer Books, 1998. This book contains dozens of articles written about the jazz giant over the course of the last six decades.

Internet Sources

Public Broadcasting Service, "American Masters—Charlie Parker." www.pbs.org. A site run by the Public Broadcasting Service (PBS) channel with biographies of people portrayed on the American Masters Television series.

———, "Biographies: Art Blakey." www.pbs.org. A site with information about one of the founders of the hard bop movement and its leading proponent for more than four decades.

———, "Classroom," *Jazz: A Film by Ken Burns.* www.pbs.org. A website about the ten-part PBS documentary on jazz with great links to music MP3s, history, biographies, chronologies, and other valuable information.

Don Crowson, "Miles Davis—A Life Story," February 2, 1998. www.nettally.com. A site dedicated to the musical and personal history of one the most innovative players of modern jazz.

Mike Janssen, "Jazz and the Beat Generation." www.litkicks.com. An interesting article describing the connections between bebop jazz artists and authors and poets of the 1950's beat generation.

Red Hot Jazz Archive, "Leon 'Bix' Beiderbecke." www.redhotjazz.com. A site dedicated to one of the greatest white jazz trumpeters of the 1920s, with sound clips, suggested reading, and links to dozens of related websites.

———, "Lil Hardin-Armstrong." www.redhotjazz.com. Another Red Hot site, this one dedicated to one of the most prominent women of the Jazz Age who composed, arranged, sang, and played piano and was also married to Louis Armstrong for a few years.

Scott Yanow, "John Hammond, Sr.: Biography." http://ubl.artistdirect.com. A biography of one of swing's most prominent promoters and producers, who discovered many great musicians.

———, "Music Genres: PostBop: History." http://genres.artistdirect.com. A site with biographies and discographies of many postbop jazz players.

Mike Zwerin, "Remembering John Coltrane—'I Can't Do Any More than What I'm Doing,'" June 11, 1988. www.culturekiosque.com. An insightful article into the music and fascinating personality of John Coltrane by a jazz musician and critic, published by the online magazine *Culture Kiosque*.

Other Sources

Geoffrey C. Ward, *Jazz: A Film by Ken Burns*. 10 episodes. Florentine Films, 2000. An excellent ten-part series about the history of jazz, produced by Ken Burns for the Public Broadcasting Service and released on VHS and DVD.

www.airto.com. A site featuring recordings and photographs of Airto Moreira, as well as an extensive biography and tour date information.

• Index •

1960's revolution, 82–83
Nirvana (band), 92

Oliver, Joe ("King"), 19, 26, 34
organ. *See* electric organ
Original Creole Band, 19–20
Original Creole Orchestra, 32
Original Dixieland Jazz Band, 22–23, 24
Ory, Edward ("Kid"), 19–20
Oxford Companion to Jazz, The (Keep-news, Milkowski), 82, 84, 85

Parker, Charlie ("Bird"), 9, 56, 57, 58, 62–64, 94
Pastorius, Jaco, 90
Payne, Nicholas, 93
Peabody Award, 93
percussion. *See* drums; rhythm
piano, 36, 56
  see also names of pianists
polyrhythm, 15
pop (music), 10
postbop, 92
Powell, Bud, 67
Pozo, Chano, 60–61
Presley, Elvis, 55
Prima, Louis, 94
Prince, 92
Prohibition, 28–29
Purim, Flora, 90

R&B (rhythm and blues), 10
racism, 21–22, 51
ragas, 77
ragtime, 8, 10, 16–17
rap (music style), 94
records, 20, 23, 26, 33–34, 68–69, 85–87
Redman, Don, 44
Reed, Lou, 85

reeds (band section), 42
rhythm, 9
  see also beat; drums; time signature
rhythm and blues (R&B), 10
rhythm (band section), 42
"riffs," 9, 15
Riley, Jim, 85
Roach, Max, 66
Roaring Twenties, 27–40
Roberts, Marcus, 93
rockabilly, 94
rock and roll, 55
Roger, Shorty, 72
Rogers, J.A., 30
Rollins, Sonny, 74, 75, 94
Roseland Ballroom, 44, 47
Russell, Pee Wee, 34

"Satchmo." *See* Armstrong, Louis ("Satchmo")
Savoy Ballroom, 44, 51–52
saxophone, 18, 41, 42, 45–47
  see also names of saxophonists
scale (musical), 56, 60
scat, 9, 34, 52
Setzer, Brian, 94
shag (dance step), 44
Shaw, Artie, 41, 53
Shaw, Woody, 75
shim-sham-shimmy, 44
Shipton, Alyn, 19, 34
Shorter, Wayne, 85
"shout" vocals, 47
Silver, Horace, 74, 75
Sinatra, Frank, 44, 55
singers, 43–44, 47, 51–52
  see also names of singers
Sixties, the, 82–83
Smith, Bessie, 33
Smith, Willie ("the Lion"), 36, 38
soul, 38, 74

• Picture Credits •

• About the Author •

Stuart A. Kallen is the author of more than 150 nonfiction books for children and young adults. He has written on topics ranging from the theory of relativity to rock-and-roll history to life on the American frontier. In addition, Mr. Kallen has written award-winning children's videos and television scripts. In his spare time, the author is a singer/songwriter/guitarist in San Diego, California.